# Superman

SUPERMAN
The Art and Science of Life Management

Robert Heller

SIDGWICK & JACKSON

LONDON

First published in Great Britain by Sidgwick and Jackson Limited

Copyright © 1978 Heller Arts

ISBN 0 283 98397 3

Photo-typesetting by Rainbow Graphics, Merseyside and Printed in Great Britain by
R. J. Acford Limited, Chichester, Sussex for Sidgwick and Jackson Limited, 1 Tavistock
Chambers, Bloomsbury Way, London, WC1A 2SG.

Contents

Introduction

This book is designed as a guide to the *real* life sciences – the knowledge and the methods which help to improve human effectiveness and happiness. It is not an encyclopaedia of the hundreds of techniques currently marketed as methods for better management of the self. Rather, I have selected from this large, growing and sometimes confusing armoury of self-help weapons those which are of proven and demonstrable worth – demonstrable, that is, to the reader.

Each chapter includes practical illustrations in basic areas of human performance; nearly all these examples can be acted on at once with immediate results. The techniques not only apply to an enormous range of activities – from eating and exercising, reading and writing, to relaxing and relating, earning and spending: they also apply at any stage and age in life. The evidence, however, suggests that interest in self-management rises sharply for the man or woman in the middle zone, from 35 to 55, when performance has to be at its highest: and when the desire – and need – to raise and maintain levels of achievement and enjoyment is often acute.

Enjoyment is as crucial a word as effectiveness. This book isn't meant to make people feel guilty about their failings; nor does it peddle panaceas. But if you want to perform better, which means to live better, there are easy ways of doing so. They are also interesting, diverting and life-enhancing. Above all, they work – and they work at any time and for nearly all people.

Anybody writing in this field is deeply indebted to many scholars and scientists. Their indispensable research and experimental work has established modern techniques and developed up-to-date understanding of ancient ways. Some of the books and papers they have written are included in the bibliography or in the text. However, I owe a special debt of gratitude to three authors I know well and one I have never met.

The latter is Dr Kenneth H. Cooper, the father of Aerobics and the main intellectual force behind the world-wide spread of running as physical and psychological therapy. His books have stimulated my interest in the whole field of the life sciences by their remarkable combination of assiduous research, common sense and basic effectiveness. Another American writer, Peter Drucker, has greatly influenced my thinking (as he has that of everybody else concerned with those matters) on the management of organizations and of the executives who staff them. He is, moreover, a living demonstration of the meaning of lucidity and insight in human thought.

In England, I met Donald Norfolk and Tony Buzan before I read any of their excellent books. Even without the latter, both men would have had a profound impact on my work. Their knowledge of the human body and mind is seemingly inexhaustible, and both have been unfailingly generous in sharing this knowledge with me. Both have also kindly read the book in manuscript: the improvements are theirs, the faults my own. My admirably expert brother, Dr Michael Heller, was also good enough to read the book in proof and to pass on his invaluable comments.

I should like to thank the following for allowing extracts and tables from their books to be reproduced: Pitman & Sons Ltd., for a series of exercises for speech and posture from *Clear Speech,* by Malcolm Morrison; Jonathan Cape Ltd., for tables on 'How to Conduct Transactions' from *I'm OK – You're OK,* by Thomas A. Harris; William Heinemann Ltd., for a quote from *The Effective Executive,* by Peter Drucker; Penguin Books Ltd., for a chart from *This Slimming Business,* by John Yudkin, and an exercise from *The Anatomy of Decisions,* by P. G. Moore and H. Thomas; M. Evans & Co. Inc., for two charts and a short passage on run tests from *The Aerobics Way,* by Kenneth H. Cooper; Sphere Books Ltd., for associations from *Speed Memory,* by Tony Buzan; Routledge & Kegan Paul Ltd., for basic vocabulary charts from *The ABC of English,* by C. K. Ogden; B.B.C. Publications for comprehension tables from *Use Your Head,* by Tony Buzan; Wildwood House for a chart from *Type A Behaviour and Your Heart,* by Meyer Friedman and Ray Rosenmann; and Tuttle, Tokyo, for exercises from *T'ai Chi: The Supreme Ultimate Exercise for Health, Sport and Self-defence,* by Cheng Man-Ch'ng and Robert Smith.

Many others have played important roles in my journey around the self: indeed, one of the fascinations of the subject is the number of people who contribute invaluable information and the number of places where it can be found. I have also had excellent assistance with the manuscript from Anne Booth. My editor at Sidgwick & Jackson, Margaret Willes, has been most encouraging and helpful throughout. Without Sidgwick's managing director, William Armstrong, moreover, there would have been no book. It was from an idea of his that Superman developed. I'm very grateful.

1. Make Your Own Superman – or Woman

Faster than a speeding bullet!
More powerful than a locomotive!
Able to leap tall buildings at a single bound!
Look! Up in the sky!
It's a bird!
It's a plane!
IT'S SUPERMAN!

THAT radio message of 1940 stirred the blood of America. Its appeal goes back to primitive man. But it is just as potent in the world of the late seventies. For Superman, read the Bionic Man and Woman – or the anthropomorphic gods of the Romans and the Greeks. Throughout history man has been painfully conscious of his physical and mental limitations. So he has invented transcendent supernatural or extra-terrestrial beings – man-like, but Supermen.

The myth-making of the centuries reflects our individual inferiority complexes. We all believe in *Superior* Man, if not in Superman. You probably think that somebody else is much stronger and fitter, much more energetic, much brighter or sexier, more self-confident, harder-working, tougher, better organized, more efficient than you. So do the men and women you envy. Nobody is immune from self-doubt – not even the mighty. Why do you suppose that Sir Winston Churchill drank too much, lived on sleeping pills and suffered black depressions?

Superman and Superior Man are both fiction. Everybody feels inferior in key respects. It's only your own feelings of inferiority which convince you that others have no sense of theirs. But the myth of Superman hides a marvellous reality: the fact that your own powers, physical and mental, are grossly under-exploited.

Of course, there's also truth in the cartoon character told by his psychiatrist not to worry about feeling inferior, because he really *was* inferior. Anybody can be outsmarted or outrun or outfaced by somebody else. But whether a real inferiority, as opposed to an im-

9

aginary one, has any importance depends on the circumstances. If you're not in a competition, it doesn't matter where you finish.

Almost certainly, you can't run a half-mile much faster than John Walker, the New Zealand ace, takes to cover a whole mile. But who's asking you to run against an Olympic champion? Or anybody else, for that matter? What's true of the legs applies to the mind. Some super-minds seem to have total recall of every fact they have ever read, while you cannot remember the title of the last film you saw. But when were you last *seriously* impeded or damaged by a failure of memory? Especially for facts like the date of birth of Karl Marx? (It was 1818, if you want to know.)

The real-life Superman is only as effective as he (or she, since sex or gender are no barrier to improvement) needs to be. There is no point, except simple amusement, in developing a faculty or skill for which you have no use, or only limited employment. But 'as effective as you need to be' almost always means more effective than you are at present. Every significant aspect of the performance of the human mind and body can be improved – without much difficulty and over most of the normal lifespan. What's more, most people do improve over time, without even being aware that they are self-improving. *Awareness enhances progress and performance.*

Why Me? Why You?

My previous books dealt with things like the true nature of management, how to make millions, and the nakedness of the investor. How did I come to write a book about this very different kind of management – the management of the self? A few years ago I didn't realize that self-management existed; let alone that this vital art is one which everybody practises; but which they would and could practise far more successfully if they managed themselves self-consciously.

In this respect, people in their daily lives are no different from successful and unsuccessful men of business whose professional lives I have chronicled. Time and again, I saw that the management mess-ups, the money-making ploys, the investment errors and the rest didn't come from outer space. Their source is *inner* space. That's the area of the personality and the mind where the heroes and anti-heroes shaped their ambitions and decided upon their strategies and tactics: and where, over and over, they either made their mistakes, or achieved what they *intended* to achieve.

Intention was the critical difference between my millionaires and billionaires and the rest. The self-made rich knew what they wanted and concentrated on that object. The failed managers had failed to think, about either their means or their ends. The stripped-bare investors begged to be plucked, because they, too, wouldn't use their own resources of mind and character. Instead, they put faith in other people – and didn't even examine their credentials.

But failures and successes both *wanted* to do well. My investor study revealed that people-in-the-mass, when faced with a set of financial circumstances, usually reacted just like a truly expert expert (which usually meant doing the opposite to what the supposed experts said). As just one example, individuals streamed from the stock markets in the United States and Britain before the crash of 1973 even while the experts were still crying up the virtues of hot stocks.

Human beings are well oriented towards what is truly best for them. Doing what comes naturally, very often, is doing what's right. It follows that inferior performance, from which everybody suffers, mostly results from impediments to natural, sensible, sound courses of action. Whatever the problem, we can generally solve it, or (better yet) stop it cold. If you allow an insoluble problem to develop, or foul up the solution, it's probably because you have unknowingly made a special effort to be incompetent.

This book actually began with the idea of producing a guide to management, as a set of techniques of self-help for managers in particular. But the specific management techniques which are of any general use don't require two hands for counting. Also, management ideas which seem universally and permanently applicable have a habit of fading away when, after the passage of a few years, somebody plucks up enough intellectual courage to examine the idea from scratch: in other words, *to think*. You can test your elementary managerial thinking power with the example given on page 12.

Thinking, as other chapters will show, is the basis of self-management: mind over matter, mind over mind. Managing yourself is the key to managing anything, and the more you have to manage outside yourself, the more you need to manage yourself. But even if you don't work in business or bureaucracies, you need to master your potential with as much urgency as the corporation man – if you *want* to. That's another key: self-management is the child of both will and brain.

The Menopausal Age-Belt

The link between will and improvement provided another source for this book. My whole interest in self-management began early in that often troubled zone between 35 and 45 when men suffer what has been called the male menopause. That's when the urban and suburban male either decides to accept fate or fight it: when past success in professional or personal life no longer seems enough, and when the future is crowding in too fast for comfort. The battle isn't only against fate; it's against age, against the long physical and mental decline from the peak.

11

Basic Thinking Exercise

Here's one exercise in basic thinking. You are trying to fix a new price for a product line – say, £1 apiece for 100,000 items, on which you will make 25 per cent profit before overheads.

Your sales chief argues passionately for a 5 per cent reduction to 95p on the grounds that it will give his sales force greater selling power – and that it's always been the firm's custom to charge slightly less than the traffic will bear.

Do you say yes or no?

The answer is at the end of this chapter.

But that decline is so slow, measured even across decades, let alone years, that the menopausal male is right not to accept it. Over most of the lifespan, physical age has no significant bearing on performance in most fields. The difference is only that the young man or woman sees less need to develop higher use of his or her potential. Although it's just as valuable for the young to achieve better performance, they lack the psychological imperative of the menopausal age-belt.

That imperative shows itself in the widening gap between the mental image of the self and the physical reality. Men do not age on their personal time-scales by ten years between 35 and 45. They try to close the psychological gap by improving their physical appearance and performance: so they jog, swim, gym, squash, bike, hike, golf – and very sensible they are, too.

The overwhelming tendency to think of yourself as much younger than you are is accurate. The psychological picture of the self is what matters most. Yet this is a hard truth to accept: that you really are as old, as young, as good, as bad, as you think you are. We all believe that some objective yardstick exists, just like a yardstick. After all, if your height is six feet, or five feet for that matter, you can't do much about it – can you? Even the Bible asks 'Who by taking thought can add to his stature one cubit?'

The short, or long, answer is that *you* can, in both the physical and the psychological sense. Physically the purchase of the right pair of shoes will alter the height, if not by a cubit – which is 18 to 22 inches – at least by enough to make a material difference. Women wear high heels for good reason. In Western society the gap between a short and a tall man is only 6 inches or so on a height of five foot six: a difference of a mere 9 per cent. As for brawn, the combination of diet and exercise can produce amazing variations, either up or down.

In any case, physical stature is mostly beside the point. Your image of your physical size may be as subjective as your feeling about your age. Big men may feel physically insignificant; small women may feel physically dominant. Being tiny or short only matters to you if it matters. Probably, it doesn't at all bother Paul Newman or Robert Redford that they dwindle in their stockinged feet. On the screen, they look tall enough, and in the flesh they quite possibly feel as tall as the camera sees them. It's not lack of inches that count – it's lack of confidence, or insecurity: the Eighth Deadly Sin.

Some Gurus is Good Gurus

Insecurity is a common human affliction. It's hardly surprising when you consider the vulnerability of a baby expelled into the noisy, dangerous, uncomfortable world outside the womb. But insecurity, like any other mental condition, can be lessened or heightened by intervention. This fact has been exploited down the ages by an endless series of experts and gurus in the self-confidence business – and much of their labour has not been in vain.

Today, there are more experts, would-be experts and pseudo-experts in this particular game than the world has ever seen. This is partly because some ancient insights have acquired new validity. But mainly it's because all supply reflects demand, as any economist (including me) will tell you. If you are churning out the greatest invention since the cornflake, but the supply meets no demand, you will sooner or later (and probably sooner) cease to churn.

The voluminous flow of works on self-improvement reflects the rise of larger groups of people who can both read and afford books; it also reflects a real increase in the anxieties and complexities of everyday life. It stands to reason that, if somebody's sex-life gives them abundant satisfaction, they won't welcome a work on repairing a fading potency or a feeble orgasm. But modern man and woman have all too many areas in their lives where they are prone to feel both feeble and fading.

This syndrome is what the self-improvers (or other-improvers) seek to exploit. Name a worry, and someone, somewhere is ready, willing and (possibly) able to cure it – for a price. If the price is only that of a paperback, the investment can, at the very worst, be written off as good clean fun. It *is* fun, too. Even a basic activity like eating can be a sybaritic delight at one extreme: or, at the other extreme, a frightened journey through a land-mined region of dietary threats.

Start the 24-hour diurnal life-cycle at any point you like – at one in the morning, say – and there's a guide waiting to steer you through every twist and trauma round the clock. You can't sleep in that first hour? Psychology or yoga can step in where pills or sleeping-masks fail to work. Move on to breakfast, and some genius has devised the perfect organic meal. It will be utterly different from somebody else's perfect organic breakfast, but never mind. So long as the chosen meal suits your stomach and your palate, who cares?

If you *don't* care, you have made an important initial discovery in self-improvement, self-management and self-development. You are an experimental population of one. The experiment is a success if it produces benefits (real or imaginary) for that one person: yourself. It doesn't matter if some crank diet is doing nothing for your health. So long as you believe that chewing raw carrots is having a terrific effect on your entire organism, it may. An imaginary benefit, true, may derive from an actual harm: you can diet yourself to death. But plenty of people can save you trouble and pain by pointing out what is actually bad for your system. The drawbacks to most self-management methods are seldom good excuses for failing to improve.

Take memory, for example. When was Karl Marx born? You should know - because I told you on page 10. It was 1818, and the only reason I know is because I once deliberately learnt it just to prove that my memory still worked. Marx was a nineteenth-century figure, and the date doubled the century. Easy. As for his death, Marx died at 65 – the normal retirement age. Add 65 to 1818, and you will never forget that he died in 1883, deeply mourned by his mistress and children. Moreover, you will remember it just as thoroughly when you yourself are 65.

The 66.66 per cent Failures

The person who blames the poor performance of his memory or his muscles on his years is just hiding behind an inadequate excuse – even if he or she has passed 60. But lifespan usually has two meanings: the working life, when actions and needs are to some extent forced on people by external circumstances, and the personal life, in which internal pressures normally make the running. The two lives are naturally mixed up. But this book is predominantly concerned with the working life.

One reason is that private life is what it says – private. I can't tell you how to improve your love-life or your relationship with your children, because I don't know what you expect from or already achieve in either. But a working life, for most people, is public: and the objectives and the necessities are visible. They also have a profound bearing on the chances of private success, not least because working success must finance private pleasures and satisfactions: but also because the man who can combine office misery with domestic bliss is not only lucky, but extremely rare.

Anyway, work mostly accounts for at least ten to eleven hours (with travel thrown in) out of a sixteen-hour waking day, meaning a good two-thirds of the normal existence. Most people who fail to get satisfaction and sense of achievement at work let their disappointment infect the remaining third of their weekdays, and their weekends as well. Even that rare man or woman who's miserable in the office but merry at home isn't a Superman, but a 66.66 per cent failure.

The object is to succeed at a much higher level, but on your own terms: to make the best of yourself - not the absolute best, because that ultimate level is never achieved, but the best possible. You never know when you've reached that point, which always recedes, like death itself. Every person at every age has a theoretical life expectancy. Similarly, the 'best possible' is always ahead. Self-management is a lifetime pursuit.

Basic Thinking Answer

Here's the answer to the basic thinking question – a subject fully explored in Chapter 6. First, the fact that the firm has always deliberately under-priced has nothing to do with the case. Forget it.

Second, the cost of that 5 per cent reduction in price will be £5,000. Since your profit is 20p a unit, you need an **increase** in sales of 25,000 units – or 25 per cent – to cover the loss: alternatively, on an unchanged price of £1 you need to avoid a **decrease** in sales of 20 per cent to come out with the same profit.

So you ask your sales' supremo if he really thinks that a 5 per cent price difference can move sales by as much as a fifth in either direction. If he says yes, find a new man.

2.
All We Have Is Us

THE most extraordinary mechanism in the world, so far as human knowledge runs, is also the most compact. A European medium-sized car weighs around 18 hundredweight, measures 170 inches in length, stands just over 50 inches high, and (at the cost of enormous expenditure on labour and manufacturing equipment) will do only three things – start, run and stop: a mere fraction of the super-machine's capabilities.

In further contrast, the super-machine is tiny: seldom longer than 72 inches, or, in the West, shorter than 60 inches. Weight varies more; 100 lb and 200 lb are both well within the normal range. But even at the top of that range, the super-machine will normally fit comfortably into a cylinder with a circumference of 50 inches. Inside this neat package is a mechanism of exquisite complexity, using many of the most elegant chemical and mechanical principles known to science or engineering, sometimes in ways so abstruse that their secrets have never been fully mastered.

Despite this complexity, and despite a regrettable lack of protection against shock and external or internal damage, the super-machine seldom goes seriously wrong during an operational span ten times as long as that of the average car. It does depend, again vulnerably, on a few critical components, whose failure will mean total failure. But the design and efficiency of these key components is so excellent that this weakness is rarely disastrous.

In any case, the super-machine can often go on working well, even if with somewhat reduced overall efficiency, after severe damage to the key components. Of these, the most fascinating is the central computer. If the whole super-machine is a compact marvel, the computer is an amazing miracle of miniaturization. It can vary in size by 100 per cent; but size makes absolutely no difference to its phenomenal capabilities. Its operational powers are more elastic by far than those of other computers. The greatest product of I.B.M. is elephantine by comparison.

True, in certain mechanical functions, such as calculation or the infallible retrieval of stored data, the super-machine is notably less efficient. But it makes up for this defect by its fantastic degree of flexibility. The super-computer can leap whole stages of data-processing at will, taking short-cuts to its destination with a brilliance that cannot even be contemplated by gigantic computing machines.

The super-computer can make analogies across the whole range of its stored data. It can communicate by sight or sound, in many variations and combinations of both, and by a number of other means, some unique. The 'house-keeping' function, ordering and storing the operating procedures, which absorbs so much of the time of inferior and larger models, is done automatically and with no difficulty at all. The super-computer's automatic routines, in fact, are as impressive as its voluntary ones. It also has the wonderful faculty, not only of acting either automatically or independently, but of doing both at the same time. Its power consumption, moreover, is remarkably low.

Looked at from the angle of this computing capacity which outdoes science fiction, the super-machine can be defined as a support system for the super-computer. The entire elaborate apparatus, seen from this viewpoint, exists to protect, nourish and house the computer and to supply such services as the computer demands.

Yet this produces an instant paradox. Since all the functions of the support system are directly controlled by the super-computer, it can just as well be argued that the computer exists for the sake of the machine. In truth, the two are inseparable. Although they can be discussed separately for convenience, the distinction is meaningless: as meaningless as 'Which came first, the chicken or the egg?'

Even the physical powers of the super-machine, which in their own way are prodigious, owe more to the skills of the super-computer than to the physical prowess of the machine itself. Like the car, the super-machine can start, run and stop. But it can't do these simple tricks especially well. The fastest speed a super-machine has ever recorded is 23 miles per hour – and that was a special model on a very short run. Normal models can rarely manage three-quarters of this speed, and over longer distances (for which the super-machine has a remarkable but still restricted range) the fastest speed regularly achieved is a mere 12 miles per hour.

The Power and the Potential

As with speed, so with power. The super-machine cannot, except in the most extreme cases, lift twice its own weight unaided, which is pathetic by the standards of many other devices, organic and inorganic. The combination of its soft casing and poor engine (in terms of relative power output) place the super-machine at a permanent disadvantage in terms of brute strength. But just as the super-computer compensates for its unreliability by flexibility, so the super-machine generally makes up for its feebleness by versatility, dexterity and an unapproached ability to couple itself with other machines.

The coupling facility enables the super-machine to move and lift with both speed and power unknown to the organic world. The dexterity is beyond the capacity of competitive mechanisms, not only because of the phenomenal computing power harnessed permanently to the machine, but also because of the superior articulation of the machine's attachments. With these, it makes contact with the materials it uses: with them, it translates the super-computer's instructions into marvellous reinforcements of its natural powers – even the manufacture of hard protective shells for its own vulnerable, soft container.

The permutations and combinations of the none too numerous movements which this marvellous machine can manage are for all practical purposes infinite. Yet most models use only a restricted number of the available skills. In this limitation, they exemplify one of the other marked and puzzling characteristics of the super-machine. This is its tendency to operate far beneath capacity.

In one respect, the machine performs much better than anybody has a right to expect. The cheapness and sparse quantities of its component materials seemingly bear no relation to what they can achieve in combination. B.A. Howard has listed the components as

> enough water to fill a 10-gallon barrel;
> enough fat for seven bars of soap;
> carbon for 9,000 lead pencils;
> phosphorus for 2,200 match heads;
> iron for one medium-sized nail;
> lime enough to whitewash a chicken coop;
> small quantities of magnesium and sulphur.

This unpromising collection of common or garden substances has been assembled, moreover, to produce a ludicrous degree of overkill. A Russian professor named Anokhin has worked out that the super-computer can make so many electro-chemical inter-connections that there is no apparent limit to its abilities: the number 1 is followed by 10.5 kilometres ($6\frac{1}{2}$ miles) of typewritten noughts.

Even in the field of physical performance, super-machines which are being pressed to the limits of their capacity usually stop measurably short of those limits. The under-performance in the physical sphere is probably not considerable in the case of the special models concerned But they stop short as the result of decisions taken by the super computer, over which its support system has little control. Still, th computer is in no position to cast any stones. Even its fabulous norma performance falls a long way short of what it can achieve with training; and its trained achievements in turn only utilize a fraction of the transcendent power represented by those ten and a half kilometres of noughts.

The super-machine is of course Man, the abnormal anthropoid. The point about performance applies quite clearly to Olympic athletes. The usual explanation offered for the improvement in records from one Olympiad to another (usually by tiny percentage margins) is that training methods and the physiques of athletes have improved. But the argument about training methods is a clear case of working backwards – justifying the means by the ends, the method by the results. The same athletes using different methods might have achieved worse, the same, or better results, for all anybody knows.

As for physique, the steady improvement applies to sports where physique is crucial (weightlifting, for example) and to those where it seems to count little (long-distance running). The truth is that world-class competitors set themselves to beat the previous best mark. So long as they can surpass that mark, they are unconsciously not concerned with how much they do it by. The amazing leap of Bob Beamon, who with 29ft $2\frac{1}{2}$in. cleared all previous long jumps by some 2 feet in Mexico City, has virtually no parallels. On the whole, when world record holders are concerned with beating each other, rather than setting records, they run comparatively slowly or throw or jump relatively short distances – unless the competition presses them further.

Second, until Roger Bannister crossed the tape, evidently in a state of total exhaustion, in under four minutes, it was generally thought that running a mile that fast was a task roughly comparable in difficulty to scaling Everest. Once the time had been shown to be feasible the number of sub-four-minute miles began to multiply until top-class runners were climbing this Everest like a mere foothill.

Mind over Matter

The difficulty wasn't all in the mind, of course. But the mental block was all-important. This is another extraordinary characteristic of the super-machine: the ability of the super-computer to produce physical results through mere nervous impulses. Medical students commonly develop the symptoms (but only the symptoms) of whatever fatal disease they are studying. Religious zealots, in extreme cases, can exhibit the stigmata of Jesus Christ. But these psychosomatic reactions, mild or severe (as with the man who metaphorically but also literally 'dies of a broken heart'), are predominantly unconscious. The super-computer is also perfectly capable of *consciously* changing man's physical manifestations.

The deliberate entry into states of apparent suspended animation by Indian fakirs is a famous example. There is no magic in this talent (so far, nobody has been able to prove that there is magic in *any* magic). The yogi's aptitudes can be developed by training, practice and concentration, just like playing the piano or swimming the crawl, until the point is reached where the performer can do in automatic fashion what was taught and learnt deliberately. The great golfer knows the correct swing: but his greatness lies partly in the fact that he doesn't have to think about the swing any more. The super-computer has been programmed to produce a perfect performance every time.

Great sportsmen do, of course, lose form; the problem is then usually described as 'getting back their confidence'. Like most commonplace sayings, this one expresses the deep psychological truth. A mental disturbance has cut across the smoothly working, well-programmed computer. Until the interference is eliminated, the programme will be less efficient. It only takes the assurance that the programme is back in working order to remove the interference. But this is plainly a vicious circle – the player plays badly because he feels badly about his play because he is playing badly . . .

The viciousness of the circle explains why afflicted sportsmen visibly 'struggle' to regain form. You can see the whole pattern of existence as a struggle between the automatic and the voluntary principles of the super-machine. The super-computer likes to set up millions of working programmes that will provide the repeated routines on which the machine thrives. But the programmes are continually being disrupted, both externally and internally, sometimes to such a degree that the computer appears to have lost control altogether.

But control over the super-machine, including the brain at its head, is essential to self-management, or to achieving any objective. We are both inside and outside the machine: it is ourselves, yet we can to an important extent operate this fabulous machine like any garden mower. It is, moreover, all we have. Other assets, like money and material possessions, are useless unless they are mobilized by the machine. The machine, moreover, can create assets, make goods, provide its own environment – and, most useful of all (to the race, if not to us personally), reproduce itself again and again.

Thinkers casting about for some explanation of human existence have even concluded that this ability to reproduce is the be-all and end-all of mankind. The theory must apply to the other animate members of the universe as well – and Darwin did indeed postulate that the chicken was merely the egg's roundabout way of creating another egg. More recently, the gene has been identified as the prime mover. The selfish gene, it's said, organizes the whole of animal life to reproduce itself, as the hereditary mechanism works its will.

All you can say is that, if this is really the purpose behind human life, it's singularly badly served. Despite an embarrassing over-supply of reproductive means (an output of 200 million sperm per man per day, and the provision in the infant female of 500 to 1,000 times as many eggs as she will ever grow), mankind does not serve its genes well. Half of all human beings fail to reproduce, taking their genes with them to the grave, and the other half (at least in the developed countries) produce very few more offspring than the one per person that simply maintains the numbers of the race.

The rest of animal creation is far better at the gene-transmission game. It isn't just because of the unique ability of the human being to take contraceptive action, either. The most children ever born to a female human, or so the record books say, is 69. That was in the last century; in modern times, the front-runner has scored 32. This low reproduction rate is especially surprising when you consider how vulnerable the new-born human is to almost any assault – and how vulnerable the child stays for long years of exposure to the world. It's almost as if nature were anxious not to overfill the earth with humans (an aim in which, in the general opinion, she has failed lamentably).

You can construct similar theories about almost any aspect of human reproduction. For instance, are the most unusual preference of humans for face-to-face copulation, their equally rare potential for year-round sex, and the apparently unique ability of the female to achieve an orgasm, all part of a plot to improve the feeble reproduction rate of nature's pet creation? All such theories argue back from what is and assume that it must be – that nothing happens without design and intention. The logical fallacy is obvious.

You're Here to Live

So you can forget the idea that you're here to serve some higher or lower purpose. You're here to live, and you've been equipped with remarkable devices and talents which can enable you to live better. Moreover, you are capable of rapid personal evolution within the incredibly slow, but continuous process of evolution of the race. As just one example, the age of puberty in the British female has come down from 15 to 13+ years since 1890. But these marked, general physical changes are rare and, on the whole, less important than the largely unchanged factors – such as the persistence of the Biblical three-score years and ten as the usual expectation of life.

From the individual's point of view, anyway, the race improvements are behind in the past, and offer no hope of benefit in those years which stretch ahead to the benchmark of seventy. And some scientists hold equally firmly that individual development has also been decided by the genes: they maintain this view with as much passion as those holding similar, but wholly unscientific beliefs in the astrological fixation of human destiny. It's undeniable, of course, that every physical particle, down to the smallest of our 50,000 billion cells, was predetermined by the 46-chromosome mechanism which gave us birth. But what does that prove?

The combinations and permutations of the 46 chromosomes alone, not to mention the 50,000 billion body cells, or even the 14 billion in the super-computer of the brain, are of such an intimidating mathematical order that speculation about them is entirely pointless. What is certain is that the hereditary material is profoundly shaped, in the sense of its final outcome, by the environmental influences which it encounters. This isn't to assert that mankind is solely the creature of its environment, only to make the all-important and blatantly obvious point that mankind cannot be understood independently of that environment.

A very clear example is the tendency of bookish parents to have literary-minded children, or little musicians to emerge from musical homes. There is an equally illustrative tendency for criminals to result from criminal parentage. In all these instances, the unknowing (whose number will include some distinguished scientists who should know better) will try to attribute the children's tendencies to heredity. But how can a child develop an interest in books unless he actually sees a book? Or in music unless he hears or handles a musical instrument? As with culture, so with criminality. The man is father of the child partly by virtue of the environment with which the former surrounds the latter.

Different combinations of genes, however, will respond differently to the same environmental stimulus. In all this, there's a profound lesson for the adult. First, the malleability of the child, the ability to be moulded by stimulus and response to stimulus, doesn't end with childhood. The organism is almost endlessly adaptive: only, the adult has the priceless advantage of being able to pick and choose his stimuli. Second, many of the limitations which appear to surround anybody's performance are not innate at all: you may well be clumsy, bad at maths and shy in company because of environmental pressures which were applied to you early on. Somebody probably told you that you were clumsy, or couldn't add up, and you were content to stick that label on yourself for ever.

This doesn't mean that nobody has limitations. Anybody can learn to add up, and almost everybody does. But basic arithmetical powers, no matter how intensively developed, will not create a race of mathematical geniuses. We all learn and master different skills at different paces, sometimes so slowly that we remain unskilled all our lives – in that particular area. Some are so astoundingly fast to learn in their special zone (like child prodigies in music or chess) that the knowledge almost seems to have been implanted beforehand.

These differences in pure aptitude can be measured, which is all that intelligence tests actually do. But environmental and other subjective factors make the results less clear-cut than the statistics on physical correlations. If you're the wrong build with the wrong physiological characteristics, you simply won't become a top or even middle-class athlete, no matter how hard you try. The physically well-rounded person, even if he's not fat, simply won't make the athletic grade.

The researches of Dr J.M. Tanner at the Rome Olympics in 1960 rubbed in the point. From the 400 metres to the Marathon, the height of competitors fell progressively from 6ft 1in to 4ft 7in, while weight came down from 12 stone 1 lb for the shorter distance to 9 stone 8 lbs for the Marathon men. No matter how hard the tall, well-built 400 metre runner had striven he couldn't have kept up with the short, wiry fellows over the longer runs. Conversely the short and wiry would have floundered far behind on a single high-speed circuit of the track.

So unconquerable gulfs do exist, and it makes obvious sense to decide what you are naturally best at, in life as in sport, because that is where the best rewards for time and effort will usually be gleaned. But for the rest, you don't have to accept the present level of performance as immutable.

Very few conditions are like colour-blindness or the sad state of being tone-deaf: not susceptible to any treatment. It is true that the super-machine develops very little in the way of new or better equipment once it has completed the magical evolution from birth to adulthood. But because the brain has grown from its initial 14oz to 3lb or so (nearly all of which, in fact, has been achieved by the age of 10); because the heart has completed its advance from under an ounce to 10 or 11oz and, along the route, has lowered its beat from the infantile 140 to the adult norm of 70; because the 43 pairs of nerves which connect the central nervous system to the rest of the machine have fully developed their amazing functional powers – none of this wonderful progress brings individual evolution to a halt.

The Famous Learning Curve

Even among the mass of people who believe that their powers steadily deteriorate from the early twenties, it's generally held with great fervour that 'experience' makes up for the decline. But experience, or the passage of time, is valueless in itself. The value only arises if the experience is translated into learning – as in the famous learning curve, first noticed when B-52 bombers were being assembled at Willow Run in the United States during the war. It was found that productivity rose at a steady pace exactly in step with every cumulative doubling of output. Everybody notices the same phenomenon about themselves: practice makes perfect, as the folk saying has it: repetition improves performance, in other words. You will find the Superman index of self-management and improvement techniques on the next page.

Another definition of learning is adaptation to the environment. We do it all the time, to the end of our days. The adaptation can be conscious or unconscious. Either way, it is the super-machine's method of obtaining the fuller use of its potential, an aim which, for those who are anxious to find an objective in life, has the sovereign advantage of being both practical and attainable. The super-machine rewards those who exploit its incredible powers. And since all we have is us, it makes very little sense wilfully to under-utilize that sole asset.

SUPERMAN INDEX

3.
The Human Machine

SINCE mind and body are one, it isn't really surprising that my interest in the first was profoundly stimulated by a discovery about the second. It happened when I was on a visit to Florida to talk to the Young Presidents' Organization, as dedicated a bunch of young millionaires (you have to be under 40 to get in and you are evicted at 50) as the world has to offer.

The Y.P.O.ers, as they like to call themselves, are devoted to self-improvement, though the uninitiated might wonder what a 40-year-old millionaire needs to improve. But it wasn't the sight of members of my audience doing deep bends in their expensive track-suits at six in the morning that inspired me. No: it was the presentation of a little, innocent-looking paperback written by Dr Kenneth H. Cooper and entitled *Aerobics;* some unknown benefactor, to whom I shall be eternally grateful, slid the volume under my door at the Boca Raton Country Club.

Now, Dr Cooper is no major philosopher, no master of the pen, nor even, for all I know, a medical scientist of great note. But in his painstaking work on getting unfit and therefore grounded U.S. Air Force pilots airborne again, the doctor did what no other man, no matter how distinguished, had done before. He produced a workable, practical definition of physical fitness – and he married it to a workable, practical measurement of the contribution which various forms of exercise make to achieving and maintaining the fit condition.

As I read this book on the flight from Miami to New York, I got some inkling of the sensations which Archimedes experienced in his bath and Newton under his apple tree. Like most people (men more than women), I had always wanted to be 'fit' and had always taken exercise in the vague hope that it was making me fitter. I had ploughed up and down the swimming baths in Greenwich Village, walked miles along the beaches at Hammamet, thrashed squash-balls whenever I had the opportunity, but I literally didn't know what I was doing, and I wasn't, absolutely wasn't, fit – not on the Cooper definition.

27

1.5-Mile Run Test
Time (Minutes)

MEN

Fitness Category	20-29	30-39	40-49	50-59	60 +
I Very Poor	16.01	16.31	17.31	19.01	20.01
II Poor	14.01–16.00	14.44–16.30	15.36–17.30	17.01–19.00	19.01–20.00
III Fair	12.01–14.00	12.31–14.45	13.01–15.35	14.31–17.00	16.16–19.00
IV Good	10.46–12.00	11.01–12.30	11.31–13.00	12.31–14.30	14.00–16.15
V Excellent	9.45–10.45	10.00–11.00	10.30–11.30	11.00–12.30	11.15–13.59
VI Superior	9.45	10.00	10.30	11.00	11.15

WOMEN

Fitness Category	20-29	30-39	40-49	50-59	60 +
I Very Poor	19.01	19.31	20.01	20.31	21.01
II Poor	19.00–18.31	19.30–19.01	20.00–19.31	20.30–20.01	21.00–21.31
III Fair	16.34–15.55	19.00–16.31	19.30–17.31	20.00–19.01	20.30–19.31
IV Good	15.54–13.31	16.30–14.31	17.30–15.56	19.00–16.31	19.30–17.31
V Excellent	13.30–12.30	14.30–13.00	15.55–13.45	16.30–14.30	17.30–16.30
VI Superior	12.30	13.00	13.45	14.30	16.30

Alternative Run Test

Run as far as you can for 12 minutes. For men, covering 1.5 miles in that time is good for all male ages from 20 to 49; 1.65 miles is excellent for the same ages. Superior means 1.77 miles or more (20-29), 1.7 or more (30-39), 1.66 or more (40-49).

For women, a good performance in 12 minutes is 1.24 miles from 20 to 49; 1.30 is excellent (1.35 from 20 to 29). Superior means 1.46 miles or more (20-29), or 1.40 (30-39), or 1.35 (40-49).

Any 1.5-mile run under 12 minutes earns 8 Aerobic points: under 15 minutes earns 6½ points. Five of the latter per week or four of the former will maintain good condition.

Equivalents to running	= 1.5 miles in under 12 minutes	= 1.5 miles in under 15 minutes
Walking (15-20 mins a mile)	4.5 miles	3.5 miles
Swimming (2.5 to 3.20 mins per 100 yards)	950 yards	850 yards
Handball/Squash/Soccer, etc.*	45 minutes +	35-40 minutes
Cycling (4-6 mins a mile)	9 miles	8 miles

*Continuous exercise.

These charts are taken from *The Aerobics Way* by Kenneth H. Cooper, published by M. Evans & Co. Inc., New York, 1970.

In his first book (he has kindly relaxed his standards since to allow for advancing age) the doctor laid it down dogmatically that a fit man could run one and a half miles in twelve minutes: and I couldn't. I could just about run a mile in nine minutes, and it cost me a painful calf injury. So I was guilty of two offences.

First, my exercise programme wasn't a programme at all. It was an uncoordinated expression of the old animal desire to take some physical exercise, no matter what.

Second, I had broken the first commandment of all human activity: which is that, before achieving anything, you must know what it is you are trying to achieve.

The Track to Enlightenment

The next stage of progress along the path, or rather the track, of enlightenment came from putting the Cooper precepts into practice. A mild and easy running programme very soon made the formidable distance of a mile seem tolerably short. My time came down almost magically to eight minutes (eventually it was under seven). Strange dents appeared in my abdomen where previously solid fat had filled in the holes. I passed Cooper's twelve-minute test, with difficulty: and then found, to my amazement, that it became routine.

That was the true revelation. No matter how much progress I had made, in time or distance, I could always make more. One summer day (you can usually run faster in warm summer than in muscle-freezing winter) I even ran one and three-quarter miles inside Cooper's twelve minutes. For what it's worth, which isn't much, that placed me in the 'excellent' category for a man of any age, let alone a 44-year-old who, a year before, could only just run a mile at any speed or any price.

The philosophical fall-out from the experience was more important even than the physiological benefit. After all, here was this body with which, after all those years, I was fairly familiar. Yet after a few weeks of very little effort – maybe twenty minutes a day – I had markedly modified its performance. After a whole year, the machine was functioning more efficiently in several crucial respects. For instance, its resting pulse rate was down from 80 to 60.

If the heart, lungs and leg muscles could respond in this dramatic fashion, what about the rest of the machine? And what about the mind, too?

Actually, there are indications that parts of the human mechanism besides the heart, lungs and muscles do respond to Dr Cooper's treatment too; however, his therapy is essentially cardio-vascular. That's to say, he defines fitness as the ability to consume given amounts of oxygen, or (which comes to the same thing) to pump blood around the system. But since the super-computer in the cranium consumes a fifth of the blood supply, it's a logical assumption that it can benefit from a fuller, freer flow.

As it happens, tests have indicated that the physically conditioned man performs standard aptitude tests with somewhat better scores than before conditioning. It hardly matters whether the predisposing factor is physical or psychological. The results are what counts. The healthy mind seems to perform better in the healthy body. So the self-improving ancients (*mens sana in corpore sano*) knew whereof they spoke.

Fit for What?

This is one answer to the cynic who asks, about fitness programmes, 'fit for what?' If your life consists mostly of one and a half hours commuting, six and a half hours at a desk or conference table, split by one and a half hours for lunch, what's the point of being able to run a mile and a half in twelve minutes?

The cynic might as well advise a man whose car is misfiring on one cylinder not to worry. The car will still travel at 30 miles per hour, and nearly all a city-dweller's driving is at that speed or below. The car-owner still won't be happy at the wheel of an unfit car: and, sooner or later, unless the unfitness is cured, the thing will break down completely.

Just as bears and other hibernating animals can live off their fat during long winters, so middle-ageing human beings can live off their earlier conditioning. I met one fat and deplorably unfit doctor who had just discovered this truth. He bought a bicycle as soon as he realized that his body, after years of satisfactory performance, was showing the signs (like shortness of breath and a creaking cough) that a medical practitioner knew to be the beginning of the end. He felt (and he was right) that it was never too late to repair the damage, and that a vigorous cycling programme would avert the threatened breakdown.

It is also true, very naturally, that physical breakdown *will* occur one day. Nobody has yet succeeded in living for ever. But you might as well try. The well-exercised human, even if genetically predisposed to coronary heart disease, reduces his chances of an attack, and improves his hopes of recovery, by virtue of his exercise. The risks of the second great slayer of men, the cerebral haemorrhage, are similarly reduced. That leaves only one major scourge–cancer. Some cancers (like those of the breast and cervix) can be caught by early screening. The fastest-growing variety of that group of disorders (lung cancer) is largely optional (all you need do is give up smoking); so the scope for warding off the evil eye and hour is greater than you may think.

The lesson shouldn't fall on deaf ears these days. Apart from the invention of new drugs, the two most significant advances in health care since the Second World War are the rapid spread of awareness that unfitness and fatness are unsatisfactory, and the knowledge that both conditions can be quite easily eliminated – simultaneously, at that. The unholy duo are linked, not because any exercise programme on its own will reduce weight (it might not), but because regular exercise does help to keep weight under control.

The mechanism can be expressed as simple arithmetic.

Suppose that you take no exercise whatsoever and ingest 3,000 calories a day. That's probably 350 calories over and above your actual need. Every twelve days, the excess calories will add one pound to your weight. Over a year you will add a couple of stone – 30lb or so. But suppose that you take a very brisk five-mile walk every day, completing the distance in an hour. That consumes the offending 350 calories, which means that you won't put on the offensive weight.

You could diet on the same arithmetic. But 1lb in twelve days is much slower than can be achieved by several nutritional regimes (of which more later); and the reducing value of the exercise will be negated, anyway, if you don't simultaneously watch your food intake. An increase in calorie consumption to 3,350 will leave you back where you started. So the fat reduction game is ancillary to the fitness one – except that you will find it much easier to meet Dr Cooper's Aerobic standards if you're not carrying, wherever you go, 30lb of excess weight about your person.

The Best Value for Money

The Cooper standards are given in the table, which is for running, the best Value for Money (or Time) among the doctor's favoured sports: running, walking, swimming, cycling, squash or handball and various kinds of stationary running or stair-climbing. He's also measured other exercises, from badminton to wrestling, but their Value for Money can be judged by the fact that three sets of tennis singles between players of equal ability, each set lasting twenty minutes, give *less* physical benefit than running one mile in eight minutes. The tennis players will feel much more tired than the runner, true, but fatigue is no indication at all of exercise value.

Using the sub-eight-minute mile as a yardstick, the other sports match up this way. Walking a mile in less than twenty minutes (but more than fourteen and a half) has a fifth of the running mile's value. So does cycling two miles in from eight to twelve minutes. A 200-yard swim in less than 6.40, but more than five minutes, is again a fifth of the running mile in terms of cardio-vascular benefit. Running on the spot for two and a half minutes, getting in 200 to 225 steps in all, counting

31

cach time the left leg hits the ground, and raising those old feet eight inches every time – again, a fifth.

That leaves the only competitive ball game in the Aerobic prime list, squash or handball. Thirty-five minutes of continuous play will match the benefits of that eight-minute mile: so you can see the strength of the Value for Money argument for running and understand the sudden appearance all over the Western world of earnest middle-aged men in track suits, pounding around the parks and highways at assorted paces. Even a two-mile jog in just under twenty-four minutes (a pretty funereal pace) gives you 7 points on the Cooper scale. Do that five times a week, and you easily meet the Aerobic requirement of 30 points for maintained fitness.

When friends suddenly turn into fitness fanatics your ideas about your own condition are invariably challenged. If you think yourself to be fighting fit, ready to take on all comers, you may be in for a shock. Even regular exercise (like my own strenuous two games of squash a week) can leave you as a gasping failure, on the twelve minute test. The two main explanations are that you are not in fact taking a 30-point level of exercise; and that you are concentrating that exercise at weekends, with little or nothing in between.

You can alleviate this problem, improving the shining hour, and the flagging body, by making use of odd moments. To earn the minimum single point on the Cooper tables, for instance, you only need to walk one mile inside twenty minutes. If you have an appointment at one o'clock, say, leave twenty minutes beforehand and proceed to your destination, by a circuitous route or directly, at a brisk enough pace to earn your point. (If your left foot strikes the ground nineteen times every twenty seconds, you will do it in a breeze.) Half an hour to kill at an airport, or anywhere else, can be passed in the same beneficial way – all contributing to the desired state of excellent fitness.

Conditioning – what Dr Cooper calls 'the training effect' – probably begins to wear off after as little as two days of inactivity, which means that from three to four exercise sessions a week (adding up to the magic 30 points or more) is the necessary ration. Magic is the word: the weekend tennis or squash player who starts to run will find his ball-game improving. As always in these matters, the reason is simple. Timing is a matter of being in the right place with the right amount of energy available to direct at the target. If you get to the spot earlier, and with greater reserves of energy, you should strike the ball better.

The self-supposed fit man who finds, from the twelve-minute test, that he isn't as fit as he thought, will probably react by stepping up his exercise to become fitter. But what about the determinedly unfit fellow? He can either react much as the smoker confronted by the facts about lung cancer and observe that we've got to die of something, sometime: or he will be tempted to do something about his condition. In contrast to giving up smoking, giving up being physically sloppy is extremely easy and involves the minimum of will-power.

You won't achieve real fitness, however, by indulging in any of the gimmicky notions, from bedroom physical jerks to isometric exercises, which seek to persuade the uninitiated that you can dispense with reasonably prolonged movement of the body, leading to energetic operation of the heart and lungs. If Dr Cooper's programme is the most advocated, and the most followed, it's only because it's the most precise and the best tried: and it really isn't at all hard. If you're grossly unfit, for example, unable to run .85 of a mile in twelve minutes in the age group 40 to 49, you start off doing a mile five times a week in under eighteen minutes – child's play.

After six weeks, your task will still only be something reasonably mild: a mile and a half, five times weekly, in 20.30. And in the sixteenth week, you will graduate to what at the beginning will seem like the dizzy heights of an eight and a half minute mile (once), twice round the one and half miles in 13.25, and twice round two miles in 19.30. The interesting point, relevant to all self-improvement, is that the distant, intimidating, impossible target comes nearer and nearer with repetition, until, when it is actually achieved, you cannot understand what all your original fuss was about.

The psychic glow of self-satisfaction, however, will be as great as if you had actually accomplished something magnificent, like beating Kip Keino or John Walker over a mile. That is part of the value of all physical or mental conditioning. It increases self-confidence to aim at and hit a target which is beyond your reach at the moment of its selection. Nor is it only the sense of achievement that makes the fitter person feel better. The improvement in circulation of the blood, the increase in physical reserves, the ability to apply more physical energy, all give rise to an improved sense of well-being – in other words, the mind does benefit along with the machine.

More far-reaching claims can be made for the benefits of exercise – and some of these will be examined in the chapter on stress, to which exercise is highly relevant. Here, our interest is mainly in the efficient operation of the machine, which is primarily dependent on the capacity and performance of the heart and lungs. If you're in the male climacteric age-belt, and haven't taken any exercise save the odd stroll for years, it won't do to belt round a running track for twelve minutes to test your condition. You won't drop dead – the system will stop you long before you can burst your heart, or any other such physiological nonsense. If somebody does suffer a heart attack on the squash court, it would have happened anyway, which will not be much consolation. But if you overdo exercise in any medical condition, you will feel dreadful.

33

Better by far to check first (preferably with your doctor – it does no harm, unless you're a raving hypochondriac, to have regular health checks, and may do good). You can also check yourself by the simple method of running up and down a flight of ten stairs, ten round trips a minute, for six minutes. That simple activity consumes as much oxygen as running a mile in ten minutes, which may help to explain why women, who mostly take far less conscious exercise than their mates, are often in better wind and limb than they apparently deserve to be.

Run up and down stairs until the heart is pumping away ferociously, then take your pulse. There are a couple in the throat if you can't find those in the wrist. After ninety seconds, take the pulse again. Timing the beat for ten seconds and multiplying by six, or fifteen seconds and then multiplying by four, will both do nicely.

Subtract the second pulse rate from the first, and then divide the difference into the first number, thus: Rate after climbing the stairs, 150; pulse after ninety seconds rest, 120; difference, 30. Divide 150 by 30 and you get 5, which, I'm sorry to tell you, isn't good at all. A score of 3 (that is, if your pulse had dropped to 100) is good, and anything under that is excellent. Score 4, and your condition is only fair; score 8, and it's terrible. What's more, you have everything to gain by improving.

Any exercise which raises the heartbeat for a sufficient period sufficiently often will do, and the above test will check your progress. But remember that it isn't possible, no matter who tells you otherwise, to attain real fitness by half an hour's exercise a week, or by physical training exercises (calisthenics) alone. Excellent programmes like the Canadian Air Force 5BX best-seller include running exercise or the equivalent. The latter, unaided, will condition the body in the Cooper sense. Where the physical jerks will help is in stretching and contracting muscles which are not used in the chosen exercise, or which are used, but which can easily turn round and bite the user if not properly prepared.

The above benefit has nothing to with effort. The languid, easy movements of yoga or T'ai Chi (the Chinese PT which Mao's children happily perform in public parks) will preserve the middle-aged citizen, or any other age group, from aches and strains just as effectively as 5BX, and with much less expenditure of energy. (Asiatic regimes are discussed in more detail in the chapter on Stress.)

The older the exerciser becomes, the more important it is to prepare the joints and sinews for their regular work-out. A sprain, strain or tear can put the victim out of action for weeks – and remember that conditioning wears off very quickly. On the other hand, the benefits of conditioning may linger on for many weeks, even for months, after the conditioned physique has been let off the exercise hook.

Beating the Black Zones

One friend of mine gave up a vigorous programme of cycling and running, yet was boasting long afterwards about how well he felt ('never better') without any exercise at all. But he admitted, under third degree questioning, that at the time his exercising had helped greatly to carry him through a rotten period, physically and mentally.

Such black zones come to most people. (Churchill actually called his 'Black Dog'.) A characteristic of the reactions of the afflicted at such times is that they become introspective, worried and obsessed about their physical condition. The obsession is part of the ailment, and both can be cured by the same simple expedient of taking exercise. But nothing is to be gained by being equally obsessive at the other extreme. The fitness fanatic is as hopeless a case as the hypochondriac.

Physical conditioning is enjoyable in itself, pleasurable in its contribution to the machine, and essential to give the machine the best chance of performing its work (and play – some pundits even claim that the conditioned body exhibits a stronger sex-drive), an investment in improving the odds that the machine's performance will continue in more satisfactory vein for still more years. These are big enough benefits to need no exaggeration, especially as they can be earned without much expenditure of time, money or will-power: once, that is, the habit of exercise has been established. The habit, like all habits, is addictive. The addict will probably feel worse if he doesn't take his daily exercise trip, even though he probably isn't suffering from withdrawal in any measurable way.

The great bonus, as I discovered, lies in proving beyond any shadow of doubt that knowing what to do, doing it, and then repeating it will bring sharp and solid improvement in a short space of time. No acts of faith are required: no mysticism is involved. In this contest of mind against matter, mind will always win. Yet its victory also proves the immense power which matter can exert over mind.

Male chauvinist pig footnote. Women have scarcly been mentioned so far. That's because the feminine principles are no different, although the physical standards are slightly lower. You'll find what Dr Cooper expects a women in 'good' physical condition to achieve on page 28. Whereas her husband will have to make, say, at least 1.45 miles in 12 minutes to be 'good' and won't graduate into the 'excellent' category until he can manage 1.65 miles, she can get by with 1.24 and 1.30 miles. In all other matters, it's a case of genuine sexual equality – and may the best woman win.

4.
The Fuel and the Fat

THE last chapter established that there is a connection between fitness and fatness. Regular exercise means a regular consumption of more calories, which, other things being equal (like not eating more to match), will avoid a regular small accretion of fat. There's slightly more to the matter. Exercise just before a meal, and the blood supply will be diverted from the abdominal region, where it likes to congregate, to supply the exercising muscles. Try to eat within an hour or so of the exercise, and the gastric sector, still short of blood, will be disinclined to digest a heavy meal.

Everybody has experienced this phenomenon, usually without knowing the physiological explanation. But it isn't always practicable to run two miles, or play a rousing game of squash, just before lunch or dinner. In any case, remember that exercise isn't primarily about losing fat. Nor is diet, although you could be forgiven, considering the mass of literature on the subject, for thinking that eating and fattening were synonymous.

Note, however, that I put the stress on fat rather than weight. The body contains a great deal of water, 70 to 80 pints in a light-medium male frame. Half the 5 pints which are lost in the normal day are put back by eating solid food (which contains water) and by internal production. If the remaining $2\frac{1}{2}$ pints aren't replaced in liquid form, the body will be lighter by that amount – which means approximately $2\frac{1}{2}$lb.

The fact that it is very easy to vary the body weight by several pounds in either direction simply by taking in or losing quantities of fluid is what gives any slimming diet so encouraging a launch – and, very often, so discouraging a letdown when the fluid loss stops. It also makes the bathroom scales an unreliable guide. The scientific dieter pays strict attention to the tape measure, which is more accurate as well as more reliable. The daily weigh-in is more valuable as an early warning system against over-eating.

But even if you're eating precisely the correct amount of calories, no more and no less, and there is not an ounce of fatty excess about your person, that shouldn't end your interest in diet. It probably doesn't, either. Almost everybody clings to some belief about nutrition, usually unscientific and generally contradicting somebody else's equally unshakable conviction.

There's plenty of room for disagreement. Time after time, nobody can state categorically that such-and-such an ingredient of diet is good or bad for the system in specific quantities or in any quantity at all. Just consider some of the current controversies over matters which, to the layman, seem as if they should be as clear-cut as the Second Law of Thermodynamics.

Double Nobel Prizewinner Linus Pauling, who knows all about the latter Law, is sure that massive doses of Vitamin C protect the system against the common cold. Pauling advocates consuming up to *four grammes* a day of this vitamin (which man, unlike cats and dogs, but like monkeys and guinea-pigs, can't manufacture himself). The generally accepted figure for the body's needs for Vitamin C is a minuscule *sixty milligrammes.*

The conventional medical view is that any excess Vitamin C (let alone an overdose of 50 times or more) gets eliminated so fast that it couldn't possibly do any good. Experiments have done little to clarify the issue: the subjects appeared to catch cold just as easily, despite the Vitamin C, but their symptoms seemed to be less severe. So the argument continues, with no benefit to anybody save the Swiss chemical giant, Hoffman La Roche, which is the leading maker of Vitamin C, and could afford to erect a statue to Linus Pauling in solid gold.

Then there's cholesterol. Some of the greatest authorities are sure that excessive build-up of cholesterol, produced by over-consumption of animal fats, predisposes the body to coronary heart disease by clogging up the arteries. Patients, especially in the States, are now as likely to undergo regimes designed to lower cholesterol levels as they are to diet because of high blood pressure. Again, other authorities are unconvinced by either the prognosis or the diagnosis – and the only clear beneficiaries are the makers of sunflower oil, margarine, etc.

Some enthusiasts urge the consumption of more fibre (by which they mostly mean bran) to compensate for the over-sophistication of modern diet. Others reckon that it's quite difficult *not* to eat enough fibre. That's also true, incidentally, of Vitamin C, if the conventional wisdom is right about the correct level of consumption. But is it right?

What's Enough – or Too Much?

In all these controversies, the tough questions are the same. What's enough – and what's too much? If human beings were rats, the questions could easily be answered. You would put the victims in identical environments, ensuring as far as possible that they were identical specimens, and give them diets that were identical in all respects save for the items under investigation. One lot could have a diet richer in animal fats, or bran, or Vitamin C, or anything else you fancied, for a period sufficiently long for symptoms of disease or breakdown, followed by death, to establish the truth.

With rats, a relatively short period on the human time-scale would enable the scientist to study the effects of diet over several generations. By comparing the results with a control group, he could then declare with considerable authority that a certain diet was harmless or harmful – to rats. But because you cannot conduct sufficiently rigorous or controlled or prolonged experiments with human beings, it's far harder to make categorical statements about nutrition.

Thus, we do know, quite categorically, that all foods contain carbohydrates or proteins or fats: sometimes on their own, mostly in combinations. But the amounts of the three that get consumed, and the balance between them, vary quite amazingly across the human race. To take just one example, an Eskimo eats over eight times as much fat per day as a member of Kenya's Kikuyu tribe, without either apparently being any the worse for it. Kikuyu and Eskimo simply have a different dietary balance.

Whatever that balance is, however, the system is reluctant to unbalance it. That is, if you cut down sharply on fats, or carbohydrates, or proteins, your intake of the other two main components of diet will also tend to fall. It's no accident that we eat bread *and* butter, beef *and* Yorkshire pudding, fish *and* chips, cheese *and* biscuits, or hamburgers which sandwich the protein in a roll of carbohydrates. Try eating either bread or butter on their own, and you will consume less of both.

This is an important clue to painless slimming; of which more later. Here the point is that while there are downward limits to the reduction of intake, especially of protein, the upper limits are unknown. Even on the lower limits, there is vagueness. One thousandth of the body weight daily is supposed to be the minimum protein need – $2\frac{1}{2}$oz for men, 2oz for women – but people have managed on much less. Whatever the minimum level, in any event, it's clearly far lower than actual consumption in the West.

I first came across this intriguing fact in an extraordinary book by an old friend, the gastronomic writer Roy Andries de Groot. In the best cookbook which ever masqueraded as a slimming guide, de Groot described how he lost 45lb in three months on something called 'the Rockefeller Diet'. The principle, worked out by the Rockefeller Institute doctors in New York, was that Western man consumed excessive protein and thus triggered off over-consumption of fats and carbohydrates as the body sought desperately to bring its diet back into balance.

The solution was to restrict protein severely, while giving the fat patient *carte blanche* to wolf down butter, cream, cakes and biscuits – all the goodies which are anathema to most diet experts. De Groot was able to quote, in support of the Rockefeller thesis, a Danish doctor, born in West Jutland, who noticed that the local farmers thrived on 'potatoes, rye bread, green vegetables, some milk and comparatively very little meat'.

History also recalls that, before the Great Hunger, the Irish multiplied and worked prodigiously on a diet composed largely of milk and potatoes, with meat no more than once a week. It was the failure of the potato crop that killed the Irish. De Groot has another ethnic group to cite, as well: the Otomi Indians of Mexico, who get their very limited amounts of protein from a cactus drink called *pulque*; just as the Chinese get much of their life-sustaining ration, not from meat, but from soy sauce – and look how many Chinese there are.

The West Jutlanders and the Otomis were the first of many such groups I was to encounter in subsequent travels around the human stomach. Among these pockets of people with peculiar eating habits, the non-drinking, non-smoking Mormons of Utah are the most over-worked specimens. But use of these special samples has two serious objections. First, the adaptation of man to his environment includes diet: in a cold northern climate, nutritional needs (like the Eskimo's for fat) won't be the same as in the heat of Africa (where the Kikuyu consequently eats less fat). Second, human inbreeding is a characteristic of these pockets of population.

So relative or absolute immunity to certain diseases, along with unusual hardiness, could be the result of confined heredity (with the whole population sharing common genes) rather than diet. That's one reason why all conclusions about dietary sins and virtues can be made to sound reasonable, and can be supported by evidence gleaned from somewhere in the whole wide world.

Kicking the Yudkin Habit?

For instance, John Yudkin, Professor of Nutrition in the University of London, has concluded that Western man and woman have become addicted to sugar. Like junkies hooked on heroin, consumers in Western lands take a 5oz fix of sugar every day, on average: almost three times as much as their poorer brethren in the human race. The wealthier nations, in fact, tend to eat more of all costly foods, not just sugar. But since sugar is stiff with calories (110 an ounce) if you cut sugar out, and don't replace it with anything else, kicking the Yudkin habit will certainly help – *but so will any cutback in any major constituent of diet, even water.*

Remember that $2\frac{1}{2}$lb loss of fluid every day? I was once dieted by a tiny, rotund, effective specialist doctor, who restricted his patients to so many teacups of liquid (any liquid) each day. As he explained it, the fat in the body stores water. Deprive the body of fluid, and it starts chewing up fat to slake its thirst. However, he didn't put his faith in water alone. There were pills of different colours, which were probably administered to forestall constipation: and there was a diet sheet which strictly regulated the intake of carbohydrates, and which I am sure was the decisive factor.

For the plain truth is that overweight people eat too much of everything, and that the awful ailments associated with too much animal fat, or too much sugar, or too much of anything, may well derive

---

The Full Nutrition Diet

Breakfast	*Calories*
4 oz (100 g) fruit juice	55
8 oz (225 g) wheat flakes	105
1 slice wholemeal bread	70
1 pint (6 decilitres) fortified skimmed milk	180

Lunch	
7 oz (200 g) steak (or other meat, or poultry)	400
8 oz (225 g) peas	120
1 slice wholemeal bread	70

Tea	*Calories*	*Supper*	*Calories*
1 slice wholemeal bread	70	4 oz (100 g) fruit juice	55
$\frac{1}{2}$ pint (3 dl) fortified skimmed milk	90	8 oz (225 g) spinach	40
		1 slice wholemeal bread	70
		$\frac{1}{2}$pt (3 dl) fortified skimmed milk	90

This diet provides all the vitamins, carbohydrates, proteins and fats required. It contains 1368 calories: a normally active man of 160 lb weight would lose about 2 lb a week on this diet. It also provides enough fibre (the equivalent of five ounces of wholemeal bread or two dessertspoons of bran is an adequate ration).

The information in this chart is taken from *The Aerobics Way*, by Kenneth H. Cooper, published by M. Evans & Co. Inc., New York 1977.

---

simply from eating too much. In rich countries, we tend to overeat, and (following the theory of dietary balance) excess of one kind is highly unlikely, in the normal organism, not to be accompanied by excess of another.

That being so, it makes more sense to worry about the total intake than about its make-up. Left to itself, the healthy body will seek to ingest the amounts of amino-acids (the constituents of proteins, twenty in all, of which nine are essential to continued life); of vitamins; of fats; and of everything else that it needs. The best-known experiment in nutritional science (since it was reported by Dr Benjamin Spock in his immortal *Baby and Child Care*) took tender infants and laid before them foods of all kinds. While the babies might go on binges with particular foods, it was observed that, taken overall, they gave themselves a balanced diet. What makes you think that you're less bright than a baby?

Average Weight of Men and Women

HEIGHT – without shoes.   WEIGHT – with ordinary clothes.

If you weigh without clothes, take off 7 lb (3 kg) from these weights if you are a man, and 5 lb (2 kg) if a woman.

Remember that weight may be 10 lb (4 kg) more or less than the average, if of heavy or of light build.

Height			Women				Men			
ft	in	cm	st	lb	(lb)	kg	st	lb	(lb)	kg
4	8	140	8	0	112	50.4				
4	9	142.5	8	2	114	51.3				
4	10	145	8	4	116	52.2				
4	11	147.5	8	6	118	53.1				
5	0	150	8	9	121	54.4	9	0	126	56.7
5	1	152.5	8	12	124	55.7	9	3	129	58.0
5	2	155	9	2	128	57.6	9	6	132	59.4
5	3	157.5	9	6	132	59.4	9	9	135	60.8
5	4	160	9	10	136	61.2	9	13	139	62.6
5	5	162.5	9	13	139	62.6	10	2	142	63.9
5	6	165	10	2	142	63.9	10	6	146	65.7
5	7	167.5	10	6	146	65.7	10	10	150	67.5
5	8	170	10	10	150	67.5	11	0	154	69.3
5	9	172.5	11	0	154	69.3	11	4	158	71.1
5	10	175	11	4	158	71.1	11	8	162	72.9
5	11	177.5	11	8	162	72.9	11	12	166	74.7
6	0	180	11	12	166	74.7	12	4	172	77.4
6	1	182.5					12	10	178	80.1
6	2	185					13	2	184	82.8
6	3	187.5					13	8	190	85.5

This chart is taken from *This Slimming Business* by John Yudkin, published by Penguin, 1970.

Your diet is almost sure to be perfectly adequate nutritionally. I've produced a table (page 40) which enables you to check that this is right (or that your eating is). But it's the other table (page 41) which is most likely to reveal deviation on your part - one that gives the standard weights for various heights.

The Overweight Greatest

This example has been taken from Yudkin's *This Slimming Business,* but is typical of many. And it's by no means gospel. For instance, Muhammad Ali, when he first fought George Foreman, weighed in at 215½lb. Since The Greatest is six foot three, that made him 26½lb overweight, according to the table: and (which hasn't always been the case) Ali was in superb shape for that duel in Zaire. But the tables show what ball-park you should be in, and your eye will confirm if you are outside the stadium.

If you are overweight, you are over-eating. Just stop the latter, and in addition to the effect that relative abstinence will have on the form, it will make you feel quite extraordinarily better. The euphoria, a feeling of light-footed springiness, won't last. This is typical of all self-improvement. The first, fine, careless rapture fades away as the system gets used to its new condition. The rapture is just a brief bonus, an extra to the general benefit of carrying less adipose tissue around.

The cure for excess eating is simple: eat less. But the standard methods, like counting calories or dropping one meal a day, are open to various objections. (On the latter point, for example, it does you no good to miss meals, and rats fed the same amount of calories put on more weight if they have one great daily gorge instead of several regular nibbles.) As for calorie counting, it's tedious and complex. It also fails to take advantage of the discovery noted above – that it is harder to eat fat without carbohydrates, and vice versa: and that protein consumption won't be so high if the other two are restricted.

In other words, you can make the body help you to diet, instead of forcing it to diet by restricting the total intake of foods – when it may be screaming for more. Like most people, I'm carbohydrate-sensitive. Give me an overdose of starches, and I part company with my target weight at once. So the obvious answer (and the one with which most doctors, and most esoteric slimming diets, end up) is to pick a low carbohydrate diet.

An added advantage is that the carbohydrate content of foods happens to be much easier to remember and count than the calories (especially since many foods contain no carbohydrate at all). Moreover, this type of diet is much easier to accommodate within a normal working and social life, which is highly important, both psychologically and practically.

'Normal social' includes alcohol in my book, although alcohol is also one of the most contentious substances in the dietary constellation. Alcoholic drinks are unquestionably foods: a straight Scotch, according to Yudkin, contains as much carbohydrate as an ounce of sweets. Since all alcoholic drinks are made by fermenting sugars, that sounds logical. But other authorities (to the eternal comfort of drinking man and woman) attribute no carbohydrates at all to most of the world's desirable tipples.

The exceptions are the sweet drinks (liqueurs, Sauternes and the richer German wines, champagne, port, richer sherries and madeiras), which still retain a heavy sugar content in the finished state. A glance at any wino on the Bowery will prove that an all-alcoholic diet doesn't fatten, however. The drunk becomes emaciated, but his diet is, of course, deficient in every nutritional need. If you're going to drink (and why not), eat – and eat well. Practical experience shows that it's possible to do both, and still lose weight and girth.

The adoption of a low carbohydrate diet like that printed here, restricting carbohydrate intake to not less than 40 grammes a day, but not more than 60, and not restricting 'dry' alcohol at all, should produce a most satisfactory weight loss. You should come down by 4 to 5lb in the first week (some people don't: every machine is different). After that, the loss should be a steady 1½ to 2lb a week.

This is ideal. Crash and crank diets are no solution. You need to effect a permanent change in eating habits. After long enough on this regime, a sweet tooth will turn lastingly sour. If you're worried that you will also turn lastingly alcoholic, follow the eminently sensible prescription of French physicians, who have laid down that seven drinks a day is a safe and moderate regime. If you don't think that's enough, then you may have more than a dietary problem.

If you've been brought up on the idea that carbohydrates give you energy (as they do), you will worry unnecessarily. The body, if it can't convert sugar and starches into the blood sugar it requires, will perform amazing chemical feats to achieve the same result from stored or eaten fats. Don't incidentally, fool yourself with the belief that some sugars (glucose, for instance) are better for you than others: the body is absolutely impartial, and converts them all into glucose, come what may.

Nor will any diet which is adequate in calories leave you short in energy. Boxers have to last up to forty-five minutes of strenuous activity (just try standing still for fifteen bouts of three minutes, with one minute's rest in between, even slugging at a stationary punchbag): and they generally stock up on protein – usually red meat – before a fight. Reg Harris, the legendary British world sprint cycling champion, came back in his fifties to regain his title after a long lay-off. He had been

The Low Carbohydrate Diet

Breakfast	Carbohydrates (grammes)	Calories
½ grapefruit	12	55
Two eggs, any style	—	160
Ham or bacon	—	90
Half slice of wholemeal bread	6	35
Coffee (black)	—	—
1 teaspoon honey	4	16
	22	

Lunch		
Clear soup	—	30
Fish or meat (7 oz)	—	400
Green salad or green vegetable (not peas)	5	30
Slice of bread	12	70
	17	

Dinner		
Clear soup	—	30
Fish or meat	—	400
Green salad or green vegetable	5	30
Slice of bread or apple	12	70
Cheese (2 oz)	—	230
	17	
	approx. 60	approx. 1,650

If you want simply to maintain weight, the normal calorie intake for a normally active man or woman is body weight in pounds multiplied by 15. This gives the amount of calories on which he will neither gain nor lose weight. A man weighing 172 lb would need 2,580 calories a day to stay put. On this diet, he would therefore have a daily deficit of around 930 calories a day, or 6,510 per week. Since a deficit of 3,500 calories would lead to a weight loss of 1 lb, he will lose slightly under 2 lbs a week. Exercise would take him over the 2 lb mark: a one-mile run (117 calories) in under eight minutes five times a week will do the trick. Additions to the diet should come exclusively from the following list of foods:

meat, bacon, offal, fish, poultry, game, sausages; eggs, cheese, butter, margarine, cream; green salad, asparagus, cabbage, mushrooms; lemons, rhubarb, yoghurt (plain).

These foods will lessen weight loss by increasing the calorie intake, but should still leave you well under the break-even point. But you should in no circumstances add to the diet from foods on the following list:

all fruit (except those above), milk, other vegetables, avocado, bananas, bread, white beans, cakes, chocolate, cottage cheese, chutney, coconut, corn, currants, dates, ice-cream, jams, fruit juices, pasta, pastry, potatoes, prunes, pickles, raisins, rice, sandwiches, thickened soups, sweets, sugar, sweet mixers, sweet wines and liquors (including port), melon.

You can drink up to seven tots or glasses a day of dry wines and spirits, and it is advisable to take a multivitamin pill while on this type of diet.

following a low carbohydrate diet of the type described here for two years.

So you don't have to maintain your past levels of starch-eating. Nor do you *have* to give up drink. But should you abstain? When *Newsweek* magazine celebrated the American bicentenary, its editors had the bright idea of beginning and ending the feature with interviews of two centenarians. One attributed his hundred years to total abstinence: the other reckoned that her daily snort had prolonged her life. Probably neither was right, except in the sense that eating and drinking what you enjoy is always the correct policy – but eating and drinking less than you can is even more correct.

The stomach is an obligingly elastic organ, although a superfluous one. We can digest food perfectly well without its services. Possibly the stomach and its elasticity were needed to cope with a stage in man's early history when meals were few and far between. Eat less, and the stomach's demands to be filled shrink, which means that your desire to fill it, your appetite, will also shrink.

The Anti-Food Devices

Another anti-food device, already mentioned, is to exercise (as recommended earlier) within an hour before mealtimes. (Exercise will also help to control the cholesterol level, if that is your worry.) It also helps to take your food and drink seriously. The more you insist on the highest quality, the less (unless you are singularly fortunate) you will eat. Pause before reaching for the tray of canapes: ask yourself, Do I really want that soggy piece of toast topped by one slice of hard-boiled egg and a truncated anchovy? The answer should be NO: it requires discrimination, not will-power.

There's still a vexatious and vexed question to answer. We all like to believe that there's some wonder-food or combination of foods that will change our lives and improve our healths. The cider and vinegar combo appears to have faded into relative (and deserved) oblivion. But Barbara Cartland, the startlingly healthy and successful 70-year-old who writes romantic novels, swears by a ration of three teaspoonfuls of honey a day. Others aren't happy without their daily dose of wheat germ or sunflower oil or muesli.

Others are obsessed not so much with the food as how it is grown. I have compared eggs from happy free-range hens with those from barbarically batteried fowl; contented Rock Cornish hens with supermarket victims; beefsteak from presumably blissful cattle with products of modern factory farms – and neither my palate, nor that of a great gourmet friend, could detect any gastronomic difference. In a just world, *pâté de foie gras* would taste worse because of the disgusting treatment of the geese from which it comes: but it doesn't. Certain additives harm the flavour, but none are at all likely to be found in concentrations that could harm anything else.

Patronage of the health food stores which have mushroomed all over the world is good in so far as the patron purchases good food. Most of the crank foods are nutritious, and none are positively harmful unless you fail to eat enough of other foods. (My own grandfather fatally undermined a formidable 80-year-old constitution by a crank diet that was deficient in protein – a hard thing to be.) I personally love honey: but I'm far from convinced, unlike the romantic Mrs Cartland, that the pollen and other wonders which I'm consuming along with the carbohydrate are doing me any special good.

I also like yoghurt, which turns out to have at least one useful property. If antibiotics are giving you an unpleasant taste in the mouth, a few spoonfuls of yoghurt dispel the taste in a few magical moments. But I'm far from convinced, here too, that a diet of yoghurt has any general blessings to offer. And conviction is the name of the game. If you have faith in your diet, you will benefit from it more than if you fret about your feeding.

So relax; set a target weight and target dimensions; if you're above the latter, reduce your intake of food; check the vital statistics at the same time every day; stabilize when you hit the targets; return to the diet when the needle on the weighing machine wobbles in the wrong direction. But remember that man is the only gourmet in the animal kingdom. I'm sorry for people like the publisher Henry Luce, who would shovel in his food inattentively, arguing that 'It's only fuel.' It's much more than that, symbolic and satisfying, rich in allusions and life-enhancing as well as sustaining. As a wise lady once sighed to me, 'Food is a great comfort.' Good food is surely among the greatest comforts of all.

5. The Ghost in the Machine

THE controversy about mind and brain, and whether there is any significant difference between the two, is one of the oldest in human thought. Even the word 'thought' is itself part of the controversy. To 'think' suggests to most people a deliberate mental activity, in which man likes to believe that he differs profoundly from other animal species. *They* only have reflexes: they don't act mentally. They 'react'.

But man is also reactive, as susceptible to conditioned reflexes as any performing dog. You can no more disentangle reflex or conditioning from 'mind', or its religious equivalent of 'soul', than you can separate any mental manifestations of any kind from the known physical structure and operations of the brain.

The big advances in recent years in mechanical (or physiological) knowledge about the brain have helped in improving mental efficiency (see the next chapter). But we aren't much wiser, on the mind/brain question, for the knowledge, say, that the brain is really two brains: that the left-hand brain is the mission control for language, mathematics, analysis, logic and so forth, while on the right sit the centres of imagination, music, rhythm, colour, etc. Soul and spirit will obviously be more comfortable on the right; but doesn't 'mind' quite plainly belong on the left? Anyway, aren't music and maths intimately linked? And imagination and language, for that matter?

The brain/mind constantly poses conundrums, paradoxes and puzzles. There's one for a start in the spectacle of the brain trying to work out how it works. There are parallels. I.B.M. uses computers to design computers. But the use of reason to analyse reason, thought to describe thought, memory to anatomize remembering – all these are circular activities. Their mysteries are a reminder, first, that the mind/brain covers much strange and little-charted territory, and second that the brain/mind has complex and useful powers of self-control, self-analysis and self-development.

The performance of the brain, left or right hand, can be modified

47

(or improved) simply by taking thought. This facility is based partly on its seemingly inexhaustible physiological powers. Not only will you only be using a fraction of its potential, no matter how much you raise its performance; but if either side of the brain is damaged, the other side (if you are lucky in the zones which have suffered) may be quite capable of taking up the load. (The most celebrated proof is Louis Pasteur, who worked on his microbes with high success and originality after his brain, so autopsy revealed, had been half-destroyed by his strokes.)

If your performance in the technical functions of reasoning, reckoning, reading and remembering, discussed in the next chapter, is poor, it almost certainly isn't the result of mental incapacity. The problem is generally the inadequate use of perfectly sound equipment. But the brain isn't only a technical facility. That is, in addition to faculties which everybody possesses, there are gifts which a few people have, but others lack entirely.

The phenomenon known as Wolfgang Amadeus Mozart wasn't amazing only because of his prodigious speed at writing down musical notation. Rossini probably wrote operas even faster (he had more practice, and *The Barber of Seville* took a scant twelve days). But while the Italian was a very great, a superb composer, he was still no Mozart. What constitutes the difference between talent and genius, competence and brilliance, the supreme and the sublime? Is it the Ghost in the Machine, in the evocative phrase of the English philosopher Gilbert Ryle?

Tapping the Latent Forces

The question isn't academic, since a great deal of the self-improvement industry revolves around the Ghost, around the idea that there are latent forces, inside or outside ourselves, that can be tapped by whatever technique is being proffered – or peddled. Some of these techniques, in their ultimate form, are stupefying by contrast with the norm; no more stupefying, perhaps, than the abilities, in the purely physical sphere, of an Olympic gymnast like Olga Korbut, but mind-boggling, nonetheless.

It's a marvellous demonstration of mind over matter to be able to meditate in deep trance, as the more revered swamis can do, for two and a half hours. But the trick doesn't get much work done. There may be more things in heaven and earth than are dreamt of in our philosophies. But what is of benefit on earth is no less important because of that. The powers of Uri Geller, assuming (a large assumption) that they are not an illusionist's tricks, are astonishing. But in practical terms, the Geller powers can only bend forks and keys, stop watches and transcribe notations; anybody reading this book can do anything that Geller can, only with much greater ease – using normal physical powers.

Faith can move a great deal; but not mountains, so far as we know. Few of us, in any case, are likely to have that much faith. But we are certain to be able to exercise direct control over the body and the brain, because we do it all the time. The Ghost in the Machine is a most obedient servant, who asks in return only two things: an adequate blood supply and sleep – to be accurate, dream-filled sleep.

The initials R.E.M. have become famous since the experiments which discovered 'Rapid Eye Movements' in sleeping subjects and established that the flickerings occurred when the sleepers dreamt – as all sleepers do, whether they can recall their dreams or not. The Ghost, it turned out, can survive more easily without sleep (that is, un-consciousness) than without dreams. You could say that in dreams the Ghost takes over, being given a free run of the physical premises for its own purposes of re-ordering, sorting and expressing the inputs of the day.

No dreams, and the Ghost goes haywire. No sleep, no dreams. So it's important to make sure of having as much sleep as you *want*. (*Need* is difficult to determine, since the average of seven hours and forty minutes conceals a vast variation.) One method of insurance is simply to sleep when you feel sleepy, instead of fighting it. Most people, probably rightly rather than wrongly, believe that catnaps are more refreshing than a much longer period of night sleep.

In practical terms, there may be no difference between nodding off in a concert and the deep meditation which a swami achieves only after many long years of dedicated training. Scientists disagree on this subject, but some do maintain that it's impossible to tell the two states apart. Either way, the crucial point is to give the Ghost time off from its normal hectic wheeling and dealing in day-to-day operations, so that it can return to the task with renewed vigour and sanity.

What is sane, or insane, however, is another of those unanswerable questions. The brain is the location of the intellect, true. But it is also the residence of the emotions, which are essentially irrational, or seem to be. Fear, jealousy and anger are atavistic forces which swamp the gentle Ghost and greatly affect its ability to go about its business. They may stem from some perfectly rational purpose: if primitive man's hackles didn't rise, he rapidly became sabre-toothed tiger-meat. And even today the rational purpose of the irrational survives.

Harnessing the Beast

Some emotional drives, like the competitive urge, unquestionably enhance both mental and physical performance. They are the bright side of the emotional coin; feelings such as grief or anxiety can either depress the brain's output or stultify it completely. (For an insight into your own depression or lack of it, see page 53.) The emotions are the Beast in the machine. The need to harness the Beast explains many of the psychological and para-psychological techniques and theories which have been so popular in this century. Just as religions offer life after death, so Freudian psychology (and its derivatives and competitors) offer life without the Beast – or with the Beast tamed.

The offer is deceptive. Even if it is possible to understand your emotional complexities, a possibility which can never be rationally demonstrated, to understand isn't necessarily to control. Anyway, many therapists and gurus argue that control of the wilder emotions is itself harmful. That's the rationale of therapeutic schools in which acting out the emotions, or abandoning the shibboleth against touching, or stripping the self naked (either emotionally, or physically, or both), is supposed to release the suppressed emotional forces.

So it will. Japanese workers probably do feel positively better after the sessions, thoughtfully arranged at their places of work, at which they can belabour dummies of their bosses. If you have a positive emotional problem, like hating your boss, it's better to do something about the problem, rather than let it fester. The more severe the problem, naturally, the higher the level of help required. Somebody whose mind is genuinely sick may well be cured by a genuine psychiatrist. But if you're not ill, very obviously you can't be cured: alternatively, you can be cured by anybody or anything.

Everybody is a bundle of sometimes conflicting, sometimes negative, sometimes downright harmful emotions. The condition is basic, like the system's dependence for survival on water (the body finds it much easier to dispense with food). Be glad you're neurotic, in other words. The dark emotional waters can be the source of vital mental sustenance. As mind needs brain, so the Ghost needs the Beast and cannot function without it.

Yet there's no doubt of the efficacy of the various fashionable neuro-psychological therapies that come and go, across the States in particular, but also across the middle-class intellectual world in general. Graduates of the Esalen Institute's encounter sessions did in many cases experience a 'spiritual' uplift, which may well have helped substantially in their practical lives. Moreover, not one of Esalen's competitors, from E.S.T. (Erhard Seminars Training) to deep meditation, has failed to help at least some, maybe a majority of those who signed on the dotted line.

It doesn't devalue these therapies to say that they fit two definitions. They combine the Placebo Effect with the Attention Factor. Whether communal (strangers thrown together) or individual (like meditation), all these therapies have elements of belonging to a club, which in turn carries overtones of tribalism and belonging. The reinforcement which the Ghost gets from comfort in numbers can be seen in everything from a

football match to a sales conference. Together the three factors – Placebo, Attention and Club – are as potent as L.S.D.

The Placebo is the most mysterious of the trio. For many decades
it's been known that patients fobbed off with sugared water or sugar pills
will recover from the trivial symptoms which they have taken to a
doctor. The word means 'I will please' in Latin. The pill-taker is pleased
with the doctor's agreement that his patient is ill, which is symbolized by
the offer of treatment, and the patient is satisfied by the mere fact of
being treated. So far, so simple; but the working of placebos is now
known to plumb deeper depths.

In the double-blind tests which have become obligatory in the
development of new drugs, patients given the harmless pills may recover
from genuinely serious ailments just as impressively as those who are
being dosed with powerful chemicals. Since many illnesses can originate
in the mind rather than the body (even diabetes can be psychosomatic),
it's not surprising that the mind can cure as well as kill. The belief in the
pill is itself a formidable therapeutic agent, and the therapeutic powers
of belief are the most convincing demonstration of the potential mastery
of the mind.

Compared to that, the benefits of an encounter session are
chickenfeed. People attending the session are like an illusionist's
audience. They have not come to see the trick fail, but to witness the
illusion working. They *will* it to work. Not surprisingly, it does. Don't
knock the Placebo Effect, however. Very few things in human life are so
helpful and so harmless. The snag is, of course, that once you know the
pill only contains sugar, it probably won't work. So, if you have a mental
therapy that operates infallibly, cling to it, and count your blessings.
Nor does it follow that, once your eyes are opened, therapies must be
ineffective. There is still the Attention Factor to consider.

We Want to Be Stroked

This factor was best, if not first, isolated in an experiment whose
fame is in inverse proportion to its use. One Elton Mayo established at
the Hawthorne plant of General Electric near Chicago that, just as
analysands respond to the attention of the psychoanalyst, irrespective of
what the shrink says, so do we all respond to the stimulus of being
noticed. Mayo's female workers raised their productivity when the
lighting was brightened; they went on improving when the illumination
was dimmed; and so on.

The guineapigs liked being tested, they responded to the clear
evidence that somebody was interested in their wellbeing and their
activities, they wanted to give the experimenter good results. The same
phenomenon stands out at any and every coaching session. It isn't just

51

that the coach gives useful guidance, but that his very attention is a source of encouragement and stimulus.

We all want to be noticed – to have our backs stroked, in Eric Berne's wonderful metaphor – and to be stroked by somebody else (a guru, a doctor, a teacher, a coach, an analyst, etc.) is best of all. But you can also pay increased attention to yourself, with equally amazing results. The good effects wear off, true, just like those of Mayo's guinea-pigs in the G.E. plant. But the benefits can always be renewed by application of the original, or different techniques, and the renewal can be an endless process.

Demonstrating the effect of self-attention is easy. Stand outdoors with closed eyes: you hear more sounds, and more clearly, than when your brain is simultaneously coping with the visual signals transmitted via the retina, a transmitter/receiver which, incidentally, is notoriously easy to deceive. The story is just the same with taste and smell. Shut the eyes while sampling a 1953 Château Latour (if you're lucky enough ever to find one again), and both the bouquet and the savour will be enhanced by your private darkness.

All meditation techniques, from prayer to the transcendental dimensions of T.M., build on the same foundation – shutting out certain areas of mental activity to produce heightened states in another sector of the mind. Successful meditation seems, as noted earlier, to shut off the computer as effectively as sleep. The difference is that the meditating computer, unlike the sleeping one, doesn't go through complex and sometimes exhausting housekeeping routines.

Quite apart from the controversy over whether meditation really does differ from sleep, or whether the Third Eye of deeply successful meditation is a figment of the imagination, it's no mean exercise in self-control to put yourself to sleep by taking thought; or rather by suppressing thought. As any insomniac will testify, that's magic enough to be going on with (see the chapter on Stress for the insomniac's charter).

It is certainly harder to shut out thought, especially if you are anxious or excited, than to exercise deliberate control over several other functions of the machine. Swamis can achieve frightening feats of control over such unlikely operations as the heart-beat. The less enlightened are better advised to start with breathing to order, which happens to be the physical basis of most spiritual regimes. Deep and rhythmic breathing under control is not esoteric by any means. But it can be just as effective as one of the powerful new tranquillizing drugs (see page 161).

Drugs pose considerable problems for those interested in control of the mind. L.S.D., heroin, opium, pot, cocaine and even good old alcohol can achieve results as startling to the mental interior as any swami or

Are You Depressed?

Everybody passes through periods of depression. It's important to recognize this state. Taking control of yourself (see Chapter 13) can help to reduce your score to the safety zone. The following test was devised by Dr Aaron Bech of the University of Pennsylvania. His 'depression inventory' is primarily a diagnostic tool for professional psychiatrists. But it is a useful guide to your own condition.

Sadness
I'm so miserable I can't stand it.	3
I'm sad all the time and can't snap out of it.	2
I feel sad.	1
I don't feel at all unhappy.	0

Pessimism
I feel the future is hopeless.	3
I have nothing to look forward to.	2
I'm discouraged about the future.	1
I'm not particularly pessimistic about the future.	0

Sense of Failure
I feel I'm a complete failure.	3
When I look back I see a lot of failures.	2
I feel I've failed more than average.	1
I don't feel a failure.	0

Dissatisfaction
I'm dissatisfied with everything.	3
I don't get satisfaction out of anything any more.	2
I don't enjoy things the way I used to.	1
I'm fairly satisfied with life.	0

Guilt
I feel I'm very bad or worthless.	3
I feel quite guilty.	2
I frequently feel bad or unworthy.	1
I don't feel particularly guilty.	0

Self-harm
I'd kill myself if I had the chance.	3
I've definite plans to commit suicide.	2
I feel I'd be better off dead.	1
I don't have any thoughts of harming myself.	0

Self-contempt
I hate myself.	3
I'm disgusted with myself.	2
I'm disappointed with myself.	1
I don't feel disappointed with myself.	0

Social withdrawal
I've completely lost interest in other people.	3
I've lost most of my interest in other people.	2
I'm less interested in other people than I used to be.	1
I've not lost interest in other people.	0

Indecisiveness
I can't make decisions at all any more.	3
I have great difficulty making decisions.	2
I try to put off making decisions.	1
I make decisions as well as ever.	0

Self-image
I feel I'm ugly to look at.	3
I feel there are permanent changes in my appearance which make me unattractive.	2
I'm worried I'm looking old or unattractive.	1
I don't feel I look any worse than I used to.	0

Work difficulty
I can't do any work at all.	3
I have to push myself very hard to do anything.	2
It takes extra effort to get started.	1
I can work as well as ever.	0

Fatigue level
I'm too tired to do anything.	3
I get tired doing anything.	2
I get tired more easily than I used to.	1
I don't get any more tired than usual.	0

Eating
I have no appetite any more.	3
My appetite is much worse than it was.	2
My appetite isn't as good as it was.	1
My appetite is no worse than usual.	0

A score of
0 – is normal.
5 – 7 indicates a state of mild depression.
8 – 15 suggests a moderate depression which may need medical treatment.

Over 16 shows a severe depressive state which probably requires professional help.

visionary has ever experienced, and much more rapidly. Take an overdose of tranquillizers, and the central nervous system may paradoxically go into an agitated crisis that changes the personality more acutely than anything demonstrated by Esalen's most susceptible visitor. But it's doubtful whether temporary poisoning can truly be equated with a genuine, unaided mystical experience.

The true mind-controller certainly disdains these artificial aids. Most of the advanced spiritual regimes ban alcohol for a start, while nicotine is equally *verboten*. It's probably significant that alcohol (a powerful depressant, which most people erroneously take as a stimulant) has never developed a cult following. That's because it is cheap, mostly legal, and easily obtained. Other drugs, although often no more effective and no less addictive, are expensive, illicit and hard to get. This purely psychological aura greatly enhances their attraction, until addiction takes over.

On the whole, mental change obtained without the use of drugs is far preferable to drug-induced or -assisted states: simply because the first involves no physical danger and can be repeated indefinitely without harm. Moreover, the heightened awareness induced by drugs may be hallucinatory. There's no evidence that drugged minds are any better at anything than the undrugged – and that includes creation. Coleridge's opium-drenched poem *Kubla Khan* is almost a solitary example to set against the serried ranks of clear-headed masterpieces.

Writers (1 include myself) often do find their ideas flowing freely when in wine, and many great artists have been notorious sots. But it doesn't follow that the ideas would be less fluent or good, or the art works any worse, if the creative mind had been placed on the wagon. Alcohol may pacify the Beast, in the happy drinker: it does nothing for the Ghost in the Machine.

The fires of creativity, in any case, burn mysteriously. We know more about memory – which isn't enough – than about inspiration. The mind of man is ultimately too complex for the mind of man to grasp, at least in the present state of information. Yet the existing knowledge is enough to guide man's footsteps into this jungle of intellect and emotion and out the other side. In the end, it doesn't matter whether human creativity springs from emotional deprivation or sheer intellectual power. Only the end-product counts.

That, above all, is what the Ghost requires – an objective towards which it can direct its strange, hallucinatory talents. The better disciplined the wayward spirit becomes, the better its unpredictable performance is likely to be. That may sound paradoxical. But we have established that the realm of the Ghost and its attendant Beast is essentially paradoxical. Maybe the question is best approached by asking, What is a paradox?

Trying By Not Trying

It's a proposition that appears to contradict itself – for example, that the worst way to relax is to strive to do so, that the essence of acting thoughtfully can sometimes be to act without thought. You can easily test the latter proposition. Confront your mind with a problem it cannot solve – a clue in a crossword puzzle, say. Here's one from the London *Times*: an eight-letter word beginning with E. The clue is 'But this book isn't about physical training.' If you haven't got the answer at once, switch your attention to something else: the name of the first President of the United States. Very often in the moment of mental transfer, the blocked answer (a name you can't remember, a memory that won't surface) comes through.

Both inattention and concentration have parts to play, in other words: and you can over-concentrate just as much as you can be too inattentive. But concentration is the quickest route to improvement: it is no accident that the great self-improving best-sellers of history, from Coué via Pelmanism to Dale Carnegie, have all been founded on forcing the self to concentrate more on itself. Coué's old immortal line, 'in every day, in every way, I'm getting better and better', is closely related to such allegedly modern ideas as 'the invisible witness': the man behind your shoulder who at your behest checks your every action, and approves or disapproves. (He actually works quite well.)

But can the Ghost derive better, richer nourishment still from outside itself? Is there another world out there, into which the mind can be plugged, a world of para-psychological phenomena, extra-sensory perception and magic? The acclamation of Uri Geller shows how deeply people feel the need to believe in some such extraneous power, il-lusionary or not. In fact, the ability of the mind to be convinced by illusion is yet another demonstration of its fantastic real powers, far greater than those we customarily harness – even though people generally feel that their brains are at full stretch. Another paradox. It can, however, be resolved by a very limited application of effort. The mind will do whatever is asked of it, literally within reason. Remove reason, and you have lost the power to control.

There's seldom anything wrong with the Ghost that a little exorcism by 'exercise' (that, incidentally, is the answer to the *Times* crossword clue, in case you're still worrying) can't cure. That's what the following chapters hope to prove. I apologize in advance for the absence of magic and mysticism. They are absent for a reason best expressed by the ancient Indian chief who goes up the mountain to die in Arthur Penn's film *Little Big Man*. Watched in awe by Dustin Hoffman, the old man composes himself to die. It starts to rain. He gets up and goes back down the mountains with the immortal words: 'Sometimes the magic works and sometimes it doesn't.'

6.
The Vital Rs

THE super-computer has an infinite number of vital functions – very few of which are taught at school, college, or anywhere else. The essential skills (in particular, reasoning, remembering, reading and reckoning), while basic to education, are not part of the educational curriculum. Yet they can all be rapidly developed and improved by deliberate use of the super-computer's own powers.

Reasoning

The greatest teacher I ever knew taught me that the most important word in the English language was 'Why?' All knowledge, he said, sprang from that simple syllable. Enquiry was the gateway to enlightenment. He was, of course, perfectly right. Knowledge is not the accumulation of unrelated facts, but the provision of the means of thought. And thinking is one of the most neglected human activities.

The importance of 'Why?' lies in its organizing principle. Observe an apple falling from a tree, and all you have seen is an apple dropping to the ground. Ask 'Why?' and (a few centuries too late) you're on the way to the law of gravity. The romantic view of the mind sees it as some kind of volcano, smouldering away most of the time, but occasionally erupting into brilliant life. The prosaic reality is that, like any muscle, the mind responds automatically and impressively to training and practice.

Both amount to discipline. For instance, where a problem exists, the obvious first step is to try to establish what the problem is. Back in the first chapter we had a simple example of deciding whether or not to cut prices in order to – what? The correct answer hinged on this insight: that the proposer of the motion was unclear, fuzzy, indeterminate about what he wanted to achieve. Once the possible objective was defined (to maximize profits), the proposal was instantly revealed as nonsense.

A better word than 'thinking', in fact, is 'reasoning'. The good and true thinker searches for a reason for his line of thought, and, in investigating some phenomenon or other, establishes a reason for his interest. In Newton's case, the reason might be that the scientist could see no empirical reason why the apple had to fall to the ground. But since all apples did fall, there had to be a reason. What was it?

The law of gravity, of course, is susceptible to proof. In human affairs, solutions rarely have the perfect beauty of mathematical logic. Take a simple fact: that, if you want to add up all the numbers from 1 to 100 (heaven knows why), you don't actually need to add them up. Add the first and last numbers in any arithmetical progression (1 and 100 in this example); divide by two, then multiply by the number of figures in the progression (100, in case you've forgotten). The answer is 5050, and it can't be anything else.

In life, as opposed to arithmetic, the celebrated line from *Jacobowsky and the Colonel* applies: 'There are always two possibilities.' The answer never comes out to exactly 5050, and it is seldom true that only one answer is possible. What the logical mind tries to do is limit the area of possibility. In this process of limitation, the magic word 'Why?' plays a vital role. The British Army, not normally renowned for its powers of logical analysis, recognized this truth long ago. Plans of attack always included, as a matter of necessity, and at the very start, the word 'Intention' (a noun for 'Why?' – the intention was nearly always, in this context, to destroy the enemy).

The importance of order and organization in thinking carries within it, as does everything else in the human machine, its own paradox. There is no doubt about the importance of order. Psychologists have long known that even the tidying of external objects, like the assorted items on top of a desk, or in a kitchen cabinet, can help to tidy and calm a state of mental confusion. The ordering seems to trigger *physically* the escape from inability to start that *mental* activity which can be called brainwork.

Any System is Better than None

Putting thoughts down on paper, making lists, structuring notes – all these are more or less systematic methods of organizing thought physically so that the mind can assimilate its progress to date and proceed, step by step, along a continuing logical progression. In this process, any system is better than none at all. Personally, I'm a numbering man. If I have 2,000 words to write, I start by writing down the numbers 1 to 20, representing that many hundred-word paragraphs.

Then I have a linear framework on which to hang a series of ideas.

A friend of mine prefers 'brain patterns', in which he draws round the nucleus of his main subject area (the use of reason, say) a series of branches and sub-branches covering all the points he wishes to include (see page 88). If you have your own working system, well and good: stick to it. But it's unlikely to be especially effective unless it imposes the essential discipline of lining up your thought and establishing a staged progress from A to B and beyond – remembering throughout that the ordering is itself a contribution to thought.

This 'linear' thinking, however, has been less in fashion lately, even though it is the rock on which much of Western civilization has been built. The very clever English writer Edward de Bono has published several books constructed around his concept of 'lateral' thinking. A famous example is the puzzle of the man who enters an elevator every time he goes home, but always exits on the 12th floor, even though his apartment is on the 16th. Yet he always goes back down from the 16th floor. Why this peculiar behaviour?

The snappy catch answer is that the fellow is a midget, who can't reach higher than the 12th button. Descending to the ground floor, no problem arises. In other words, it's not really a logical problem (like the sum of the numbers from 1 to 100): it's a joke. De Bono is an expert on jokes as an intellectual activity, and jokes, in this context, are not to be laughed at. They do exemplify one extremely valuable attribute of the brain – its ability to be non-linear, to leap (sideways or laterally, if you like) to an incongruous but apposite thought.

A wise veteran once remarked to me that all jokes are the same: an unexpected outcome to an expected or predictable situation. 'Who was that lady I saw you with last night?' is a predictable, ordinary question. 'That was no lady, that was my wife' is the unexpected answer. Inspiration sometimes does appear to have the same quality. Sir Alec Issigonis had to find some way of fitting an engine under the bonnet of his Mini car without sacrificing his predetermined idea of the car's length: the unexpected response (unpredictable only because nobody had done it before) was to turn the engine *sideways*: now, there's lateral thought with a vengeance.

Whether this inspiration was truly a non-linear idea is another matter. It could have been arrived at along a strictly linear route. But suppose that this, or some other innovation, was clearly a lateral leap. Is the implication that all thinkers should positively strive to be disorderly, to encourage their brains to leap away from the linear?

At one time a technique of mass disorder, known as 'brainstorming', was in vogue. A number of people concerned with (and supposedly expert in) a problem area would meet to chuck into the hopper any thoughts, no matter how outrageous or fanciful, that came into their heads. It is not recorded that this undisciplined method has achieved any startling success at any location where it has been tried. The whole approach smacks of desperation. Anyway, any useful ideas that were stormed from the brains could only pay off when translated into logical, linear development by orderly, non-storming brain processes.

In the field of invention, success has come far more often to those seeking a means to an end (a problem in search of a solution) than to those who have spotted an interesting scientific or technological quirk and wondered what to do with it (a solution in search of a problem). So never abuse linear thought. Without the ability to follow a straight line of thinking from premise to conclusion, beginning to end, mankind would never have advanced very far from the ape stage, and without the same ability, very little can be accomplished in our own day and age.

The Origin and the Objective

It follows that you must choose the right place to start and the right place to end, the Alpha and Omega, the Origin and the Objective. The military, with their stiff and formal approach, had the right idea (you will find a civilian version on page 61). Any thought process has to start from an objective, and to proceed by analysis. Different mental methods, however, are required for different stages.

In the beginning, the analytical stage, the essential step is *knowing which question to ask*. A simple example was the one given in the first chapter. The correct question (page 12) was not 'Should we continue to shade our prices?' but 'How does the cost of price-shading match up to its benefit?' Once the right question had been established, the problem was child's play – you could say that it solved itself, which a properly posed problem almost invariably does.

All complex problems can be reduced to simpler proportions, sometimes very simple ones. The clue may be to split the conundrum into component parts, which in turn usually depends on first establishing what the problem really is. Take the immortalized Israeli raid on Entebbe. Once the military operation was shown to be feasible (question: Can we get enough troops and firepower to Uganda with enough surprise to free the hostages?), the Israelis had three possibilities, which is one better than Jacobowsky's ration.

The three were (1) to give in to the terrorists' demands; (2) to stand pat; or (3) to launch the military operation. Only the third alternative met the Israelis' prime objective, which was to free the hostages without releasing the terrorist prisoners and meeting the kidnappers' other demands. If the military blow had not been feasible, or had failed, the failure of thought or execution would have lain entirely on the military side. The civilian decision, given the military appreciation, was impeccable.

59

As a contrast, consider the disastrous landing of airborne forces at Arnhem. Here it was less a question of the wrong questions being asked than of none getting posed. The operation did appear to offer solutions to problems (How can we bring the unused airborne armada into action, and keep that bloody Montgomery quiet?). But the problems were hardly relevant to the real question of how best and fastest to win the war against Germany. Inevitably, Eisenhower and the Allies got the wrong answer to a question which had never been properly phrased.

The path to knowledge, and knowledgeable action, starts by asking a question about a question – Is it the *right* question? That in turn can't be answered without knowing what the real objective is. In the case of Arnhem, as noted, that was to complete the defeat of a shattered German army with the optimum combination of speed and safety. As Cornelius Ryan pointed out unarguably in his posthumous *A Bridge Too Far,* the correct military target, in accordance with this objective, wasn't Arnhem, but the strategically vital port of Antwerp.

Ryan's view (and mine) can always be dismissed as hindsight. But the dismissal represents sloppy thinking, too. Backwards is the only way in which we can look at the past. It is poor logic to excuse failure, your own or anybody else's, on the grounds that everybody makes mistakes (which is all that the hindsight sneer means). True, it isn't particularly clever to re-fight the battle of Waterloo (or Arnhem) years after the event. But it is particularly stupid to repeat the same errors which past failures – or sometimes past successes – display for your instruction, free of charge, and free of pain.

There are only two questions to answer for those who want to avoid their present Arnhems and win their future Entebbes. One, the first and foremost, we have already stressed: 'What is the objective, or why am I doing this at all?' It is closely followed by 'What are the alternatives?'

Each of the alternatives must be tested out against the facts as they can best be established. Not only that: they must, to be accepted, pass the 'fail safe' test: or, 'If this plan goes as wrong as it possibly can, what will happen, and will we be able to live with the results? Will they be worse than those of doing nothing?'

Decisions can usefully be divided into those that must be taken at once; those that must be taken, but not yet; and those that don't have to be taken at all. Often mistakes of the most grievous kind fall into the last category. (Arnhem was one: Ike actually didn't need to launch any such operation at that juncture.) If a decision must be taken immediately, never procrastinate. The delay seldom improves the decision, and may make a successful outcome impossible. But it is plainly foolish to take any decision until you have to – apart from anything else, that reduces the chances of the decision taking itself: meaning that a properly analysed and simplified problem will very often present its own unique solution as

Basic Action Planning

All thinking about what to do, or not to do (which equals making a decision), depends on answering these questions:
1 What are my objectives? (Intention)
2 What do I know about myself?
   ...and about others who will affect the outcome? (Information)
3 What means do I have to meet the objectives? (Resources)
4 How do I propose to use the information and resources to execute my intention? (Method)
5 How will the planned method be carried out? (Implementation)

This simplified model is basic, but needs to be supplemented by the six-stage analysis suggested by Peter Drucker.
1 **Classify the problem.** Is it generic; or exceptional and one-off; or the first of a new class of problems?
2 **Define the problem.** What are you dealing with?
3 **Name the specifications.** What requirements or conditions must the solution satisfy?
4 **Decide on the ideal solution.** What would be the best possible course of action before any compromises (which are usually inevitable) have to be made?
5 **Build into the decision the action to carry it out.** What action must be taken, and who has to know about it?
6 **Set up the feedback.** How is the decision being carried out? Are the assumptions on which it is based appropriate or out-of-date?

The information above is from *The Effective Executive* by Peter Drucker, published by Harper & Row, New York, 1966.

a result of the analysis and the simplification. That was true of Entebbe; Arnhem, improperly analysed and unnecessarily complicated, was the opposite.

Nonsense Under Our Noses

However, it's wrong to assume (as politicians and business managers commonly do) that decision-taking is the only kind of thought which people need to practise. The last paragraph introduced the key word 'analysis', with good reason. Some of the greater lunacies in human life stem from failures of analysis: not from false decisions on how to correct a fault, but from incorrect understanding of what the failing is. All of us, in all walks of life, miss glaring examples of nonsense under our noses – usually because of preconditioning.

If the following examples are taken from medicine, this isn't because I have any special disregard for doctors, some of whom win my warm admiration. The selection of these cases arises because the problems are clearly delineated, and because a highly trained profession has devoted endless hours to those problems. Which makes it all the harder to explain the mysterious case of the cuts – cuts and abrasions being presumably about the most common ailment faced in hospitals and surgeries all over the world.

Until recently any cut of moderate severity or worse was festooned with lint and bandages like the corpse of some mummified Egyptian. The big idea was to keep air, germs and dirt away from the suffering wound. *Nobody asked the obvious question.* Did the protection produce more rapid and certain healing of the wound? Once the question was asked, the answer, embarrassingly enough for the practitioners of the past, was an emphatic negative.

The ambient air, it suddenly appeared, was good for wounds, not bad, so the mummy's dressings were abandoned for vestigial strips of sticking plaster. Simple mistakes in simple medical practice, however, are not the end of the story. Medical scientists base much of their work on statistics (the most famous instance being the correlation of smoking with lung cancer). But the proper use of statistics depends on the illuminating power of intelligence. Here doctors often fall into the abundant logical traps which lie in wait for all figure-lovers.

For instance, the great debate among the psychologists about whether or not intelligence is determined by heredity is of crucial importance to society. If low intelligence is genetically determined, as the hereditary school maintains, there isn't much point in trying to educate the intellectually blighted - like, specifically, the American Negro. Or is there?

Forget that Sir Cyril Burt, the greatly esteemed British psychiatrist, apparently cooked his figures on studies of identical twins, and take his statistics as gospel. Do they show what Burt and his disciples wish to show? He claimed to demonstrate that 80 per cent of intelligence is inherited, the rest being determined by environment. Now, a middle-class child of impeccable environment scores 120 on a I.Q. test. According to the great Burt, 80 per cent of that very passable score derives from the child's genes. In other words, if the environment had been mentally paralysing, like that of a Negro in the poorest and deepest part of the Deep South – this same brain would have scored 96, just below the human mean.

The analytically untrained mind spots the 80 per cent and unhesitatingly translates it to mean 'overwhelmingly': intelligence is 'overwhelmingly' transmitted through the genes. Yet what Burt's figures prove isn't that inherited mental faculties are beyond improvement. Not at all: the statistics show clearly that environmental development can make all the difference between an academic and non-academic intelligence, or, moving down the scale, between normal and sub-normal. The Burt case also proves that for successful analysis you must challenge everything (in this case, actually, you should begin by questioning whether I.Q. test results really correlate with 'intelligence', whatever that is).

Even the human tendency to take assumptions for granted, without realizing the logical danger, doesn't cover the whole range of thought-halting processes. Another medical example is the prevalence of large hospital wards (called Nightingale wards in Britain, since they date back to the Crimean War). The prevailing wisdom holds that the large ward economizes on nursing staff (because one nurse can see down a large room containing up to forty patients) and develops a medically helpful community spirit.

It would never have occurred to me to question these principles until I heard some sceptic arguing precisely the opposite. Private hospitals or hospital wings with single-patient wards, he observed, have less nurses per patient. What's more, you need fewer beds (and thus less construction expense) in a single-room hospital. As usual the idea is only paradoxical because the contrary, the general assumption, is based on an absurdity. No sooner is the absurd assumption exposed than the paradox becomes an obvious truth.

The typical ward cannot contain men and women, general surgical patients and children. Since society will never oblige by sending a mix of patients exactly compatible with the mix of beds, a substantial number of the latter (up to a third in practice) are bound to be unoccupied. With single rooms, the mix can far more easily be varied to meet the actual supply of patients, and the number of excess beds required will fall. As for the nursing, two-thirds of the patients in hospital, noted my sceptic, are fit enough to look after themselves in any case, and would probably prefer to. You can, moreover, keep an eye on the seriously ill just as easily through a window in the door, or by opening the latter, as by looking down the length of a long, intimidating ward – whose inhabitants, to round off the story, would probably get much more communal uplift from a dayroom than from a Nightingale monstrosity.

The point of the ward controversy is not so much whether singles are right, multiples wrong, but rather that the question of the truth was not raised for decade after decade. The suppression of question and reason creates error. The human tendency is to take the given fact, or what exists at present, as unalterable, which means that it is not challenged, tested anew and again. It is as if a shopper never asked for meat to be weighed, never asked its price, never counted the change. She might become very popular with her butcher; but she would probably eat very expensive meat.

Failing to test all propositions may similarly increase your popularity, because people hate to have their received views, or their prejudices, attacked. But the failure may prove to be expensive – like the extra costs of building too much hospital space to hold too many beds to be served by too many nurses. There is no God-given truth about what exists. It is there because it is there, not necessarily because it is right.

The thinker is far from helpless or hopeless when it comes to finding the right test. Simply ask what knowledge would prove a proposition one way or another, and see if that information can be found. The magic question – Why? – is also essential. The enquiring mind is like a detective searching for clues (to establish what actually happened) and for proofs (to confirm his deductions from the clues). Take the proposition that children of low-grade intelligence at one extreme, and of high-grade intelligence at the other, should be educated at special schools. Before the detective can test the idea, he must know why segregation is adopted. If the answer is that these two extremes of school children do better educationally in segregated conditions, then a trial can be devised. (It will show, incidentally, that the low-grade children suffer rather than benefit from association only with each other.)

Always Heed a Hunch

Analysis is the route by which ideas can be deliberately arrived at and determined. If the military-type approach seems too mechanical, allowing too little room for hunch and inspiration, it's not an important objection. The mind can move or think deliberately or instinctively, just like the body. Sometimes, playing a game, the athlete takes aim with care and forethought; at other times, the machine swings and clicks into place seemingly effortlessly, almost as if its owner was superfluous. But exactly the same computer routine has been run: the difference is primarily one of speed. (You can test your own intuitions by the example on the page opposite.)

Hunch and inspiration don't fall from heaven like manna, or, in the form of visitation beloved by *New Yorker* cartoonists, from one of the nine Muses. The mind can only exploit what the mind contains. Creativity consists of making connections within the mysterious physiological world of the brain, which the latest research visualizes as less like a computer than an underwater forest of waving fronds and luxuriant tendrils. A hunch springs from connections made without the connecting mind's conscious knowledge: it should never be ignored. Like any other idea, it should be tested. But a 'gut' feeling, even though it has nothing to do with the intestines, does convey an urgent message – so urgent that it has short-circuited the deliberate mental processes. That's why it should be heeded.

But inspiration is not enough. To use another musical example (because the composition of music is the most abstract of all mental processes, yet at the same time one of the most exact), take Wagner's inspiration of writing a four-part musical drama on the old folk saga of the Nibelungs, bound together by recurring and interwoven themes, and ending (like the Ring of its title) where it began. A choice of pure genius. But its working out over the years - the decades, in fact - required mental mechanics of various orders, from the highest to the lowest, as well as further visitations from those non-existent Muses.

The nature of those mechanics can be seen from some of the more advanced mechanical devices invented to help thinkers. One such is the decision tree (page 66). Where there are several alternatives, you list them and follow through the consequences of taking any particular decision. Where the consequences are uncertain, you judge the probabilities: you're 70 per cent sure that such and such will happen, say; or only 60 per cent; or maybe you haven't the faintest idea. But the process should come up with an answer indicating which of the possible courses of action is the most likely to meet your target.

Plainly, the value of these exercises depends entirely on the strength or weakness of the assessments. Get your probabilities badly wrong, and the answer, however many digits it contains, is actually zero. But the mind is always making decision trees, just as it constantly makes lists of 'pros and cons' - a much simpler method of trying to break out of

---

Basic Intuition Exercise

You own a business that sells fresh lobsters. The trouble is that they never keep more than one day, so that any unsold stock has to be thrown away. You also know that in every five-day week, your sales will bounce about erratically. One day you will sell 10, another 20, another 30, another 40, another 50 – but you never know which day. To complicate matters still further, your supplier insists on a whole week's deliveries being ordered in advance, always in tens and for the same amount per day. They cost you $5 apiece, and you can sell them for $9.

Without pausing to think, say how many lobsters you would order for daily delivery: 10, 20, 30, 40 or 50?

You'll find the answer at the end of the chapter.

How to Analyse Decisions

Step-by-step analysis helps by making clear all the consequences and factors involved. Drawing a decision tree forces you to be precise – as follows:

You have to decide whether to stay in your present house (market value £25,000*)
OR
Buy another new, ready decorated, nearby for £35,000; you will have to provide £10,000 from cash resources
OR
Stay, but redecorate and improve for £5,000*, which you are sure will be re-couped at least half in the market value*.

The correct decision, financially speaking, will depend on the value of the alternatives in a year's time. The highest capital appreciation you can imagine is 25%*: the lowest 10%*. You also believe that the maximum rise is more likely than the minimum by 60-40 (the asterisk means these are only estimates).

Here's the Tree:

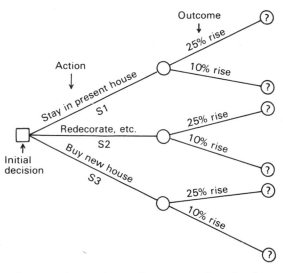

You need to work out the end-year worths: the first step is a table.

	Initial property	after 25% rise	after 10% rise
S1	25,000	31,250	27,500
S2	27,500	34,375	30,250
S3	35,000	43,750	38,500

However, this omits the £10,000 cash which will still be unspent if decision S1 is taken. Moreover, that £10,000 will earn £500 in interest if safely invested. If decision S2 is taken, there will be £5,000 in cash, plus £250 in interest. If decision S3 is chosen, the £10,000 will be included in the value of the house. So the revised figures are:

	after 25%	after 10%
S1	41,750	38,000
S2	39,625	35,500
S3	43,750	38,500

The analysis is still not over, because you can't be sure of the 25% which makes S3 look best. Remember that the 25% rise will happen, you think, 60% of the time: 10% will happen 40% of the time. So you need some sums:

	after 25%	after 10%	cash
S1	31,250x.6	+27,500x.4	+10,500=18.75 +11+10.5 =40.25
S2	34,375x.6	+30,250x.4	+5,250 =20.625+12.1+5.25=37.975
S3	43,750x.6	+38,500x.4	+0 =26.25 +15.4 =41.65

The worst course is to redecorate. There isn't apparently much to choose between the new house and the old. But look back at the tree. Its branches can continue. If you add on another year on the same assumptions, it's very clear that S3 will go further ahead. If it's a 25% rise in house prices, that must clearly far outdistance, given the £10,000 gap between the values, the 5% rise in the equal amount of £10,000 cash, even with nil inflation. Also, the old house will need redecorating *some* time.

As you'll see, quite a deal might depend on your ranking of probabilities. The rule is simple: Dead certain = 100; Absolutely impossible = 0; Could go either way = 50. You locate other possibilities between these fixed points – thus: Just possible = 10; Just possible that it might not happen = 90; Just more likely to happen = 60; Just more likely not to happen = 40. That leaves 20, 30 and 70, 80 for the more problematical negative and positive categories.

You might still decide on staying put for other reasons, like wanting to keep your cash available or liking the living room. You can put numbers to these preferences, in just the same way that you can measure probabilities. Thus, the factors in the decision might be:

A Financial outcome   C Character of house
B Availability of cash   D Inconvenience of moving

You attribute values to each factor. You award 40 points in all, say, and divide them: A = 15; B = 7½; C = 7½; D = 10.

indecision traps. In this well-known trick, the undecided mind lists under 'pro' the arguments for a certain course of action and under 'con' those against. The longest list wins.

If the winning decision is still deeply unpalatable, then the decision-taker (or non-taker) at least knows where he stands emotionally. The same test can be applied slightly more easily by tossing a coin and seeing whether you accept its decision. However, there's a considerable chance that in compiling pros and cons, the mind will instinctively load the outcome in favour of the direction it truly wishes to follow. In any case, the exercise of running through the relevant factors for and against is itself valuable, and a precaution against sloppy or incomplete thought.

Thought is incomplete unless it comes to a conclusion. That is the whole purpose of selecting a purpose – to direct thought towards an outcome. If you are 'cudgelling your brains', unable to find any solution to a besetting problem, you are (as the metaphor suggests) simply beating yourself to no good purpose. Something is intrinsically wrong in the approach to the subject-matter, or possibly in the subject-matter itself. There's a splendid proof of this from the life (and the pen) of this century's most famous thinker – the philosopher Bertrand Russell.

Russell came across what he called the paradox of classes in June 1901, when he was busily at work on his most important philosophical book, *Principia Mathematica*. His problem turned out not to be new, merely a version of the antique logical chestnut, dating back to the ancient Greeks: the one about Epimenides the Cretan, who says that all Cretans are liars. If his statement is true, it must be false, for Epimenides is not lying. If his statement is false, it must be true, for Epimenides is lying.

Russell could not resolve this type of contradiction. 'Every morning I would sit down before a blank sheet of paper. Throughout the day, with a brief interval for lunch, I would stare at the blank sheet. Often when evening came it was still empty . . . the two summers of 1903 and 1904 remain in my mind as a period of complete intellectual deadlock.' Russell, in the same passage of his autobiography, has the answer to the deadlock. 'It seemed unworthy of a grown man to spend his time on such trivialities.' So it was. Like the problem of the dwarf in the elevator, the case of Epimenides the Cretan is artificial. It can be resolved by the Gordian knot method: since nobody lies all the time, Epimenides cannot be stating a general truth, but the fact that he is lying now doesn't mean that he always lies.

Just as Alexander cut through the Gordian knot with his sword, so the super-computer, properly used, cuts through what is trivial and superfluous and deals with the heart of its real problem. This doesn't

Basic Intuition Answer

The correct answer to the lobster test is 30. Drawing up a small table will show that ordering 10 lobsters will lose 150 sales at $4 profit each: at 20, the loss is 60; at 30, the loss is 30. The waste in these three cases is 0, 10, 30. Order more than 40, and the loss climbs: since 10 wasted lobsters are worth more than 10 sold, the financial results must deteriorate. The worst answer is 50.

Based on an exercise in *The Anatomy of Decisions*, by P. G. Morre and H. Thomas, published by Penguins, 1976.

mean pouring scorn on speculative abstract thought of the kind which preoccupied Russell at that time. Many concrete contributions (including nuclear physics) have developed from speculative thinking of the highest order. But for most of us, the super-computer has practical work at hand. Cudgelling the machine is ill-treatment: small wonder if it responds by seizing up entirely.

Remembering

Few human accomplishments win more admiration than a super-memory. A 'photographic' memory is the one intellectual asset that is sure to be universally admired; although actually there's no such thing. Anyway, the connection between an excellent memory and general mental prowess is very loose. Some brilliant memorizers are brilliant at everything else, some not. Some brilliant minds have brilliant memories, some don't.

However, nobody can 'photograph' a page of a book at a single glance and then reel off the page word for word. In the first place, as the section on reading will observe, the eyes can't do it. That makes the question of whether the brain could absorb the page simultaneously and instantaneously somewhat academic. The brain is constantly absorbing every fact, sensation, sight that enters through ear, eye, touch, taste, and so on – true. It may well, somewhat superfluously, store the lot. But none of the senses is a perfect recorder, and the brain can only remember what it is imperfectly given.

Its capacity for total absorption (which is not the same as total recall, another much-advertised but non-existent human gift) could account for the weird ability of uneducated men to spout strange tongues when under the influence of drugs or hypnosis. (The theory is more convincing than the idea that their eternal spirits are returning to previous existences as shepherds in Attica, or whatever.) The ability of the entranced brain to produce memories not available in the conscious state is evidence for the total absorption concept. Certainly, nobody has yet succeeded in exhausting, even greatly exploiting, the memory's power of retention and retrieval at the conscious level.

Nor do many people exploit, or even exercise, the memory's readiness to be consciously directed. Like your legs, the memory will become more efficient with exercise, and will atrophy with neglect. Properly directed, it will soak up any facts it is asked to absorb, and regurgitate them to order. This proposition is not only true, but demonstrably so. Yet most people, plagued by their own forgetfulness, find the concept amazingly difficult to believe.

That's because, from schooldays onwards, we expect memory to function automatically, with no assistance except repetition. As it happens, repetition is an essential memory technique, but neither the sole one nor even the most powerful, if used on its own. In combination with other techniques, repetition becomes a magic wand. But take any paragraph on this page – this one, for example – and see how accurately you can recall the words after as many as ten readings out loud. Unless you have a trick or trained memory, you are unlikely to score well.

The Shopping List Trick

Try a simpler trick. Would you find it easy to memorize a shopping list of ten items? In fact, you won't bother – you will write it down. That is an important point about memory, including trick memory: there's no virtue in memorizing the entire *Encyclopaedia Britannica* if you have a copy on your bookshelves. Memory should be used when, for reasons of time, convenience or command, it is useful. The shopping list is purely for training purposes.

Untrained, you will almost certainly require considerable time and trouble to memorize in their correct order ten items of any kind. The ten I'm about to list aren't mine. They represent the shopping of Tony Buzan, an English expert who, you might say, has forgotten more about memory than I can remember. His items are: bananas, soap, eggs, glasses, bandages, matches, washing-up liquid, toothpaste, shoes and tomatoes. Now, the only interesting thing about that list is that I wrote it down from memory, with only one mistake, after a lapse of several months. How did something so useless stick so firmly in my (I like to think) extremely busy mind?

The trick was accomplished by the crucial device of association. Memory, scientists have established, is associative – we remember one thing by linking it with others, so that any human memory is a complex of linkages which makes the D.N.A. molecule look positively simple by comparison. Associate *deliberately,* and you can easily remember anything, even Buzan's ridiculous shopping list.

Here is an adaptation of the associations which Buzan provided in his book, *Speed Memory.* What do bananas and soap have in common? Both are slippery objects, beloved by cartoonists and film-makers for making patsies fall flat on their faces. Imagine yourself stepping and slipping, left foot on a banana skin, right foot on a bar of soap, with eggs and glasses (both fragile objects) in either hand. Naturally, as you fall, they break.

The broken glass cuts your hand, which you have to bandage. To destroy the bloody bandage, you set fire to it with matches. The fire gets out of hand: you can't find a fire extinguisher, so you use something which looks like an extinguisher – a plastic squeeze bottle of washing-up liquid. A small flame still sputters, so you grab a smaller squeeze container, one of toothpaste. As you squeeze, some of the paste falls on your nice, new shoes, so you step back in irritation and tread on a tomato, slipping – and starting the whole sorry saga all over again.

At this point, if you're like everybody else I've played the shopping list game with, you will either be giggling helplessly or have lost patience completely. But recover your patience and, without looking back, write down as many of the ten items on that list as you can remember – in the correct order – using the associative story as your clue. My 11-year-old daughter had them all off pat the next morning, even though she had pooh-poohed the whole business the evening before. My secretary got eight out of ten, simply as a result of typing the saga.

You should have scored well – but if you still don't believe in the efficacy of association, try this list: apples, butter, cups, gloves, cigarettes, shampoo, shaving soap, socks, cabbage and screws. The whole passage about Buzan's shopping list shouldn't have taken more than one or two minutes to read. Give yourself two minutes on the second list, without association or any other device save repetition, and see how you score. Then wait quarter of an hour, while you read a book or kick the cat, and try both lists again. If I'm right, association will win hands down.

Suppose that the point about association has been proved. What help is that? Do you have to construct fantastic rigmaroles every time you want to remember something? Not necessarily, although when using association in this way it does help, as Buzan stresses, to be fantastic. Outlandish things are easier to recall, so it helps to be absurd; his other rules are to exaggerate associations: to incorporate movement (the man slipping on the banana skin and the soap) and to use substitution (the washing-up liquid for the fire extinguisher is an example) in order to strengthen associations. The rules are sound, and, as you should already have demonstrated, they work. Yet why do so many people, adults as well as children, resist the technique?

The answer, as with most mental malfunctions, is probably conditioning. In school, where all learning by heart is by rote, success is marked by recall, doing it the hard way; and it somehow seems less virtuous to use a trick – even though mnemonics are favourite devices of scholars for learning essential facts, and have been since the days of the ancient Greeks and Romans. They used so-called 'topical mnemonics', in which you remember things by locating them in the rooms of houses in an imaginary town. Thus, to remember 1440, when printing was introduced into Europe, your Graeco-Roman technique is to place a book on the 40th quadrate (or memory place) of the fourth room in the first house in your town.

The Associative Fix

Frankly, that's just the kind of superfluous sophistication you'd expect of a primitive society. 'Thirty days hath September' (another typical, but non-topical mnemonic) is much more sensible. All mnemonics, subtle or simple, are no more than a form of deliberate association. But resistance to the idea is so inbred that people will argue, for instance, that it's no use their creating an associative story (like the bananas-to-tomatoes one), because they would forget the association itself. That misses the whole point – the act of association fixes the memory, and once the memory is fixed, you will very likely never need the association again.

Until I discovered this device there were two numbers – one belonging to a bank account, the other to a telephone – that I could never recall. Some mental block, arising no doubt from some suppressed anxiety, always interfered. It took just a few minutes with Buzan's book to destroy those mental roadblocks permanently. Yet at first I passed by this particular portion of the book, because it seemed even more irrelevant, and much less fun, than the shopping list. Don't repeat this mistake.

The technique is to write down the numbers from 1 to 10, and to compile lists of words to fit the numbers – using either visual or aural associations. For instance, you could use parts of the body for a visual association: 1, finger; 2, eyebrow; 3, ear; 4, eye; 5, curl; 6, fist; 7, nose; 8, navel; 9, neck; 10, mouth. These links may ring no bells for you, other than doubts about my mentality. It doesn't matter – make your own list, starting with pencil for 1, say, and heading off wherever you like.

No matter what route you follow in your associations, it can be guaranteed that (a) you will from memory and at once be able to recall the list in the correct order (b) you will be able to repeat it perfectly in reverse (c) you will be able to give the right symbol for any number, and the right number for any symbol, again at will. As Buzan points out, this is no mean mental feat in itself.

The same acrobatic performance will follow just as automatically from a sound list, associating the numbers aurally. For instance, sun for 1; then 2, shoe; 3, tree; 4, door; 5, hive; 6, sticks; 7, heaven; 8, gate; 9, line; 10, pen. Again, make your own list, since your own associations will be more powerful than any borrowed from somebody else. But don't imagine that you are merely playing a useless memory game. The exercise opens the door to serious remembering – of anything.

Any list of objects, ideas or people, or whatever, up to ten can be fixed in the memory by association with your ten symbols. Any number can similarly be retained by using the symbolic link. The phone number over which I had a blockage was 9580. Once I thought of bees tracing a bee-*line* to a *hive* which they entered through a *gate* carrying *nothing*, the number was fixed in mental cement. The blockage vanished, and (as promised above) I never had to refer to the little associative picture-story again.

This use of pegs is basic to conscious exercise of memory, and probably to most demonstrations, on stage or in life, of phenomenal memory powers. Stanislaus Mink von Wesnnssheim – now, there's a name to conjure with, or to remember, for that matter – was the Newton of this particular science. In the middle of the seventeenth century Stanislaus invented what is still the supreme peg system, the Major. Early in the next century the Englishman Dr Richard Grey did for the Major system what Einstein achieved in Newtonian physics. As a result, you can provide your mind with as many as a thousand pegs by converting numbers into verbal symbols.

Without going into its full detail, in the Major system the figure 2 is 'n'; 4 is 'r'; 5 is 'l'. So 245 equals 'nrl', which might suggest the word 'normal'. This provides an easy and immediate way of remembering that particular number. But it is also one of a series of pegs so numerous that it will cover any conceivable memorizing of lists for most conceivable purposes. If the 245th item is the Mozart opus of that Köchel number, you work out an association with 'normal' - and, hey presto, you can astound your friends with musical knowledge for ever more.

Memory is a Living Tool

These advanced techniques aren't needed for the executive or everyday life. The purpose of describing and practising memory devices is because they provide so convincing a demonstration that the memory, like the rest of the mind, is a living tool, which isn't frozen into immobility with the end of formal education, and which doesn't fall into decrepitude as the years advance. Those who complain that their memory has deteriorated with age (as most people do) are describing a process of atrophy, not degeneration. But the atrophied mind, like the atrophied muscle, can be reactivated by use. In any event, the degree of atrophy is usually much exaggerated.

The unexercised memory is by no means totally idle. Each of us performs remarkable feats of remembering in the ordinary process of going about our business. You may have inexhaustible, instantly retrievable information about the organization in which you work, the technology you mainly employ, or the hobby which is your major interest. Not only do these memories get fixed by association (you link the name of a subordinate, say, to occasions on which you've worked together), but repeated use has the same effect. Here the processes are automatic. If you want to memorize material which is more than a simple list, however, repetition, too, can be organized.

According to Tony Buzan, the retention of learned material is at a higher level, not just after you have learned it, but when a few minutes have passed. On the other, worse hand four-fifths of the detail of your learning is lost within twenty-four hours. The right way of exploiting these contradictory discoveries is to review what you have learnt after a time interval which is one-tenth of the time spent on the initial study. In other words if you've been studying a document or a language for an hour, wait six minutes, then run over the material again.

The theory is that you will then retain the learning for ten times the initial study period: in this example, ten hours, when you review again. If you're lucky, the study material will be securely retained from then on. If it seems to be escaping again, review at fourfold intervals: taking the same example, the next review comes after forty hours – a couple of days, say, then eight days, and so on.

Actually, an hour is an abnormally long period for unbroken study, judged by the evidence accumulated by Buzan. The memory recalls more of what it harvests at the start of a study period, and somewhat more of the material learnt at the end. It follows that the more periods of study you fit into a given time-span, the more high-recall points there will be. So Buzan recommends that you find your ideal period of concentration (usually from twenty to forty minutes) and intersperse those periods with rests of five minutes or so, during which you do nothing in particular. Stare out of the window, twiddle your thumbs: it doesn't matter, so long as you allow the super-computer to go about its business of ordering and absorbing the information with which it has just been fed.

This refreshing pause has an analogy in the organization of time, which we discuss in Chapter 7. Like the principle of memory by association, it requires some conquest of inhibition for acceptance. Man is so inured to the idea that nothing is achieved save by effort that it's hard to accept that a two- or five-minute spell of idleness actually enhances learning. There is only one antidote to the inhibition: try it and see. As with the mnemonic memory devices, the eating will prove the pudding.

The territory surveyed in this chapter covers most of the situations which the adult mind has to explore. The short period- rest- review process will greatly assist in mastering a foreign language: especially if you add to it the knowledge that a thousand words is a very substantial vocabulary. On pages 76-77 you will find the key words in Basic English. There are only 850 of them. Translate them into any other language, and you have the basis of fluency. Start with the words which are similar to English (like *Wort* and word in German, *visage* and visage (or face) in French). Then move on to the unlike words, using either one of the systems mentioned above, or the study and review technique.

THE BASIC VOCABULARY

These 850 words, or their equivalents in any language, cover the majority of requirements for most normal communication. The vocabulary is a quick test of your knowledge of foreign languages.

OPERATIONS, etc. (100)

come	send	off	all	but	now	so
get	may	on	any	or	out	very
give	will	over	every	if	still	tomorrow
go	about	through	no	though	then	yesterday
keep	across	to	other	while	there	north
let	after	under	some	how	together	south
make	against	up	such	when	well	east
put	among	with	that	where	almost	west
seem	at	as	this	why	enough	please
take	before	for	I	again	even	yes
be	between	of	he	ever	little	
do	by	till	you	far	much	
have	down	than	who	forward	not	
say	from	a	and	here	only	
see	in	the	because	near	quite	

THINGS 400 General

account	chalk	direction	front	language	name	prose
act	chance	discovery	fruit	laugh	nation	protest
addition	change	discussion	glass	law	need	pull
adjustment	cloth	disease	gold	lead	news	punishment
advertisement	coal	disgust	government	learning .	night	purpose
agreement	colour	distance	grain	leather	noise	push
air	comfort	distribution	grass	letter	note	quality
amount	committee	division	grip	level	number	question
amusement	company	doubt	group	lift	observation	rain
animal	comparison	drink	growth	light	offer	range
answer	competition	driving	guide	limit	oil	rate
apparatus	condition	dust	harbour	linen	operation	ray
approval	connection	earth	harmony	liquid	opinion	reaction
argument	control	edge	hate	list	order	reading
art	cook	education	hearing	look	organization	reason
attack	copper	effect	heat	loss	ornament	record
attempt	copy	end	help	love	owner	regret
attention	cork	error	history	machine	page	relation
attraction	cotton	event	hole	man	plain	religion
authority	cough	example	hope	manager	paint	representative
back	country	exchange	hour	mark -	paper	request
balance	cover	existence	humour	market	part	respect
base	crack	expansion	ice	mass	paste	rest
behaviour	credit	experience	idea	meal	payment	reward
belief	crime	expert	impulse	measure	peace	rhythm
birth	crush	fact	increase	meat	person	rice
bit	cry	fall	industry	meeting	place	river
bite	current	family	ink	memory	plant	road
blood	curve	father	insect	metal	play	roll
blow	damage	fear	instrument	middle	pleasure	room
body	danger	feeling	insurance	milk	point	rub
brass	daughter	fiction	interest	mind	poison	rule
bread	day	field	invention	mine	polish	run
breath	death	fight	iron	minute	porter	salt
brother	debt	fire	jelly	mist	position	sand
building	decision	flame	join	money	powder	scale
burn	degree	flight	journey	month	power	science
burst	design	flower	judge	morning	price	sea
business	desire	fold	jump	mother	print	seat
butter	destruction	food	kick	motion	progress	secretary
canvas	detail	force	kiss	mountain	produce	selection
care	development	form	knowledge	move	profit	self
cause	digestion	friend	land	music	property	sense

THINGS 400 General

servant	structure	wave
sex	substance	wax
shade	sugar	way
shake	suggestion	weather
shame	summer	week
shock	support	weight
side	surprise	wind
sign	swim	wine
silk	system	winter
silver	talk	woman
sister	taste	wood
size	tax	wool
sky	teaching	word
sleep	tendency	work
slip	test	wound
slope	theory	writing
smash	thing	year
smell	thought	
smile	thunder	
smoke	time	
sneeze	tin	
snow	top	
soap	tough	
society	trade	
son	transport	
song	trick	
sort	trouble	
sound	turn	
soup	twist	
space	unit	
stage	use	
start	value	
statement	verse	
steam	vessel	
steel	view	
step	voice	
stitch	walk	
stone	war	
stop	wash	
story	waste	
stretch	water	

200 PICTURED

angle	coat	knee	screw
ant	collar	knife	seed
apple	comb	knot	sheep
arch	cord	leaf	shelf
arm	cow	leg	ship
army	cup	library	shirt
baby	curtain	line	shoe
bag	cushion	lip	skin
ball	dog	lock	skirt
band	door	map	snake
basin	drain	match	sock
basket	drawer	monkey	spade
bath	dress	moon	sponge
bed	drop	mouth	spoon
bee	ear	muscle	spring
bell	egg	nail	square
berry	engine	neck	stamp
bird	eye	needle	star
blade	face	nerve	station
board	farm	net	stem
boat	feather	nose	stick
bone	finger	nut	stocking
book	fish	office	stomach
boot	flag	orange	store
bottle	floor	oven	street
box	fly	parcel	sun
boy	foot	pen	table
brain	fork	pencil	tail
brake	fowl	picture	thread
branch	frame	pig	throat
brick	garden	pin	thumb
bridge	girl	pipe	ticket
brush	glove	plane	toe
bucket	goat	plate	tongue
bulb	gun	plough	tooth
button	hair	pocket	town
cake	hammer	pot	train
camera	hand	potato	tray
card	hat	prison	tree
carriage	head	pump	trousers
cart	heart	rail	umbrella
cat	hook	rat	wall
chain	horn	receipt	watch
cheese	horse	ring	wheel
chest	hospital	rod	whip
chin	house	roof	whistle
church	island	root	window
circle	jewel	sail	wing
clock	kettle	school	wire
cloud	key	scissors	worm

QUALITIES 100 General

able	fat	material	same
acid	fertile	medical	second
angry	first	military	separate
automatic	fixed	natural	serious
beautiful	flat	necessary	sharp
black	free	new	smooth
boiling	frequent	normal	sticky
bright	full	open	stiff
broken	general	parallel	straight
brown	good	past	strong
cheap	great	physical	sudden
chemical	grey	political	sweet
chief	hanging	poor	tall
clean	happy	possible	thick
clear	hard	present	tight
common	healthy	private	tired
complex	high	probable	true
conscious	hollow	quick	violent
cut	important	quiet	waiting
deep	kind	ready	warm
dependent	like	red	wet
early	living	regular	wide
elastic	long	responsible	wise
electric	male	right	yellow
equal	married	round	young

50 OPPOSITES

awake	left
bad	loose
bent	loud
bitter	low
blue	mixed
certain	narrow
cold	old
complete	opposite
cruel	public
dark	rough
dead	sad
dear	safe
delicate	secret
different	short
dirty	shut
dry	simple
false	slow
feeble	small
female	soft
foolish	solid
future	special
green	strange
ill	thin
last	white
late	wrong

This chart is taken from *The ABC of Basic English* by C. K. Ogden, published by Kegan Paul, 1935.

In another application, suppose that you have a speech to give and wish to impress the audience by speaking without notes. Chapter 8 explains how to compose a script-less speech: each section will hang on a key phrase. Using a simple set of pegs, you can easily memorize the ten or so key phrases, from which the sections of your speech should hang perfectly, to the amazement of all who listen. In much the same way, you can memorize an apparently unrehearsed submission to a meeting. The important thing to remember (and this feat of memory needs no aids) is that such tricks are not only elementary but easy. No great effort is required for substantial reward.

That by no means exhausts the possibilities for the organized associative and retention techniques. But random association also has a vital part to play: for instance, in remembering names and faces. The problem here is that, for nervous reasons, the mind tends to freeze when confronted with a stranger and that stranger's name. You don't actually take it in. (In much the same way, the mind cuts out when expected to speak in an imperfectly understood foreign language. You know perfectly well that *Tisch* is the German for table, but your fright shuts off the relevant mental connection.)

An entertaining routine in Buzan's book is designed to solve the name problem. When introduced, you try to *listen* to the name. Whether you heard it or not, you ask for it to be *repeated*. If the name is at all curious in sound, you ask how it is *spelt*. You then in subsequent conversation make a point of *using* the name ('Herr von Wesnnssheim here was just saying'). If the name is really odd, you ask its owner to *explain* the origins. By the time you've been through all that, you should have at least one social embarrassment avoided for ever.

In simpler circumstances, merely use association. Make a link between the name and the face: if a man called Sharp has a pointed nose, you have an easy connection. The trick is only to perform the conscious step of memorizing. Its reverse is to hope (usually against hope) that your memory, without deliberate aid, will do whatever you require of it. You will pull a muscle that is presented with an effort for which it is unprepared. Likewise, your memory will fail you unless it, too, is trained for its essential task.

Reading

The connection between good reading and good memory is very obvious, but seldom made. Without the ability to call up sufficient vocabulary, the reader can't understand; without the power to retain some of the material he has read, the reader will gain only transitory benefit from a book, paper or poem – or any other form of writing. Despite the explosion of visual images in our time, especially through television, the global village of Marshall McLuhan's invention is still animated largely by the written word. And writing has no value, except to the writer, until it has been read.

The link with memory extends to performance. The powers of memory are under-exploited because of under exercise and bad technique. While most people read enough to keep their reading faculties reasonably fit, they read badly. As with memory, the remedies are simple, but psychologically hard to accept, because they fly in the face of folklore and habit. These in turn are based on what seems to be obvious, but is in fact wrong. For instance, you've read a passage and not understood it fully; obviously, you improve your comprehension by going back over the sentences again.

Or you're particularly anxious to concentrate on and master a piece of writing; so you obviously read it with special care and deliberation, taking more time than usual. Both these are common reactions. Both happen to be totally misguided, as elementary tests have proved. Readers who felt they had not understood a passage have been questioned about it, then allowed to re-read the portion and questioned again. The improvement in their scores was negligible. Similarly, the same kind of test has shown no appreciable loss of comprehension as reading speed rises. On the contrary, if speed improves because of improved technique, the reader should comprehend and retain *more*, not less.

However hard you find it to believe, the test scores show that 'regression', or going back over material again (and even again) only gives an extra 3 to 7 per cent of comprehension. The bad habit, however, slows down reading very much more. The slow reader who reads everything twice halves his speed. Just eliminating this one defect will of itself substantially lessen the time taken over reading. But it won't make

79

the subject into a fast reader. That means somebody who reads markedly faster than the average – and the average is something between 250 and 300 words per minute (w.p.m.). Most of the time, unless the material is very easy, you will be nearer 250 than 300.

The objective of a course in fast reading (such as those attended by dedicated self-managers from President John F. Kennedy downwards) is to raise the maximum speed by an average four-fifths, without any loss in comprehension. That means that your normal 250-300 w.p.m. range becomes 450-540. To put that into practical terms, a reasonably long book might be 100,000 words long. You can certainly hope to cut the reading time from around seven hours to three and a half hours – and this assumes (which I certainly don't) that you have to read every word.

Those who have followed and believed the story so far may still have reservations on the comprehension front. Surely, if you spend seven hours mulling over a book, you must absorb more than if you zip through it in a mere three and a half? Part of the trouble is that most of us exaggerate our powers of comprehension, anyway. It pays as a start to test both your reading speed and the amount of your reading that you retain. It so happens that this paragraph and the two before add up to 350 words. Finish, go back to the beginning and read the three paragraphs again. Note that I'm giving you the benefit of regression – so your score on the comprehension test should be higher than normal. Off you go, not forgetting to time yourself over the course, naturally.

If it took you one minute twenty-five seconds to read the three paragraphs, that's about par for the course. A minute is moving towards a good reading speed, but there is, of course, the matter of comprehension as well. You will find sixteen questions on the passage on page 83 with the answers, and the meaning of your score, on the other side. This gives you the base on which to build, or the measure against which to plot your future progress. The principles of progress, moreover, aren't the subject of ardent controversy; the nature of reading is well understood by everybody – except most readers.

The Fixation of the Eye

For a start, most of us believe that we can read in a continuous sweep of the eye. We don't, and we can't. The eye can only take in words by fixing upon them. If it really did sweep past, it couldn't take the words in at all. Our eyes proceed from fixation to fixation by small, swift movements known as 'saccades', so small and so swift that we cannot spot them. But watch a television performer reading from a telprompter, and you should be able to detect the tiny flicker as the eye moves from one group of words to the next.

Once you are aware of this basic optical principle, an immediate improvement in reading habits is presented on a plate. Discover by experiment how many words you can comfortably cover in a single fixation, and then deliberately use your eyes in that knowledge – at the same time, refusing to regress, however great the temptation. To be usefully technical, regression means deliberate re-reading because you feel you have not taken in the material. But many readers, including me, are tempted to 'back-skip', in which they go back over words or lines by some kind of unnecessary automatic reflex.

The elimination of regression and back-skipping won't win the war. But this preliminary engagement takes you a long way towards final victory, which is impossible otherwise. The difficulty is only psychological. You must overcome the conditioning which persuades you that re-reading, going over it again, produces a worthwhile improvement in understanding, and you must defeat the twitchy reflex which checks your essential progress from fixation to fixation. These two triumphs of mind over eye will of themselves immediately improve the word-per-minute score.

What's more, they are the only bad habits you need worry about – another flat statement that flies in the face of old, wrong lessons. As a child, you were probably told off for following the words with your finger, or reading aloud silently to yourself. In fact, the moving finger is one easy aid in avoiding the backward transgression of the eye. Better still, moving the finger faster will automatically speed up the forward fixations, and that means faster reading. As for mouthing the words inwardly, a trick known as sub-vocalization, the experts agree that it does no harm, whereas trying to eliminate the habit (by humming, whistling or counting while reading) does no good to anybody.

If you're a really laborious sub-vocalizer, then you have a problem. But it will disappear as your reading generally picks up speed. Of course, if your vocalizing isn't sub, but loud, then reading in general, not reading fast enough, is your difficulty, and one which needs attention. But there's evidence that even when skimming (of which more later) at speeds of up to 60,000 w.p.m. the odd word gets sub-vocalized as they all flash past in a stream of verbiage (in a tightly-printed book, that means turning a page every second).

For the non-skipper, the key to speed turns out to be the same in principle as winning a track event at the Olympics. There are only two variables in running: the number of strides in each minute, and the length of each stride. A phenomenon like the Cuban Juan Guanterero, with a 9ft stride, will cover the ground half as fast again as an ordinary 6ft strider, even if the latter's legs move at the same speed. The trained athlete, of course, also strides much more rapidly. In just the same way, a fast reader fixates a greater number of words at one time, and moves more rapidly from one fixation to the next.

81

The memory expert Tony Buzan has a simple exercise for fixing your attention on your fixations. Cover nine pages of a shorthand notebook with numbers, two columns per page. Put two-digit numbers on page one; three-digit numbers on the next two pages; four digits on the next two; five-digit numbers on the next two; and finish up with six-digit entries. Go back to the beginning, cover up the first column of numbers, then briefly expose each in turn, for no more than a split second; when it's covered again, write what you remember of the number in the adjacent space.

If you can get right through to the last six-digiter with a 100 per cent record, you get the fixation prize. From then on, reading more efficiently is a matter of practice. A good speed-reading course will do more for you than you can manage on your own (that is a general principle of self-management: the self, oddly or not, nearly always does better with help). But an improvement of 30 per cent, from 250 w.p.m. to the respectable zone of 325, should be obtained by a slow reader from these general hints alone, and still more from the exercises on page 86. And that is before entering into the highly profitable area of selection, gutting and skipping. If you're reading *War and Peace,* you won't want to miss a single word. But most writers – especially in business, alas – are a long way from Tolstoy.

The 100 per cent Cut

The most crucial of the just-mentioned trio is selection. After all, if you decide that you don't need to read the memo, paper, article or book at all, that cuts the reading time by 100 per cent. You cannot always achieve this perfection, and won't want to, of course. But it is elementary practice, with a book or something like a learned paper, or even a magazine article, to look at the beginning and the end, to see whether or not you are likely to glean much reward from the middle. A book will normally have a contents page, which may not be very informative. But the book will also usually have an introductory chapter, just as a learned paper will have a preamble, or a magazine article an introductory paragraph.

Anything written can be absolutely counted upon to have an ending. Some authors obligingly sum up all they have to say in a passage headed 'Conclusion'. In an earlier chapter I mentioned the finding that even in the processed-food paradise of the West, it is difficult, provided you eat the right kind of bread, to consume insufficient fibre. This information was passed on to me by my friend, the osteopath Donald Norfolk, who had obtained it from a whole book on the question of fibre in the diet. As he pointed out, the conclusion was so positive that it really pre-empted the need to read the book.

Comprehension – How Good is Yours?

1   What is the gain in comprehension from regression?

2   What is regression?

3   What is the average reading speed?

4   Name one famous fast-reader.

5   What is the objective of a fast-reading course?

6   What is the fast reading speed range?

7   What length was suggested for a reasonably long book?

8   How many words were in the passage?

9   What did I certainly not assume?

10   How much comprehension should a fast-reader lose?

11   What do most of us exaggerate?

12   How should you start to improve your reading?

13   Why should your score on this test be higher than usual?

14   What's the result of reading everything twice?

15   How long should a reasonably long book take to read?

16   What should you not have forgotten to do?

Answers

1   3 to 7 per cent.

2   Going back over material again.

3   250-300 words per minute.

4   John F. Kennedy.

5   To raise maximum speed by an average four-fifths with no loss in comprehension.

6   450-540 wpm.

7   100,000 words.

8   350.

9   That you have to read every word.

10 None

11 Our powers of comprehension.

12 Testing reading speed and retention.

13 Because you had the benefit of regression.

14 Halving the potential reading speed.

15 Three and a half hours.

16 Time how long the passage took to read.

100 per cent comprehension is excellent; but you are quite likely to have got half the questions wrong. Using the exercises on p. 86 should improve both speed and understanding.

These tables are taken from *Use Your Head* by Tony Buzan, published by B.B.C. Publications, 1974.

In less sharply defined cases, the introductory and concluding paragraphs will provide a quick and usually reliable guide to how much of the intervening material you want to read, and how you are going to read it. Don't run away with the idea that gutting and skipping are easy: they are harder work than word-by-word reading, because of the high degree of concentration required. But if a full reading is not necessary, or not possible for lack of time, then there are two basic choices. You can cover all the material lightly, or just some of the material, by omitting whole chunks, or by reducing the number of fixations.

Chunk omission can be done by reading down the centre, or one side, of the page, thus limiting the fixations to one per line. Not only will the area of direct visual coverage give you most of the sense, but peripheral vision will pick up more. An alternative is to zig-zag, covering the page from left to right, then right to left, with the angle of the zigs and the zags depending on your ability to take in the sense. Another method is to enclose the number of words you can comfortably encompass inside a circle – Buzan recommends one formed between the forefinger and thumb – and to move the circle along faster and faster until you achieve the maximum useful speed.

In all the above approaches, you are still trying to cover most of the material. But it's a usable truth that, just as introductions and conclusions tell you a great deal of what you want to know about a book, so the first and last sentences of paragraphs, and the first and last paragraphs of chapters, tend to be especially informative. By using this knowledge, you can again cut the amount of material to be covered, while still picking up the essentials of the book, its intestines, so to speak. This gutting, in turn, will be greatly reinforced if supplemented by taking notes – then you can recover, review or refer to the material with much greater ease.

Do SQ3R and PQRST mean anything to you? They didn't to me until I met Buzan. Both describe study methods and are organized uses of the techniques I've mentioned. Either you Survey the material, Question what you wish to get from it, then Read, Recite and finally Revise. Or you Preview the material, ask the same Question, and Read before you Summarize and finally Test your knowledge. Buzan believes both to be inadequate, and says that you should approach study by Preparation and Application, both being divided into four parts. Preparation has a great deal to do with the use of time, the subject of a later chapter. Application divides into Survey, Preview, Inview and Review.

All these stages are closely related to the techniques already discussed. The Survey and Preview combined cover the glance over the introduction, study of the contents, flick through the pages (Buzan adds the inside and outside cover and all the material outside the regular

Exercises for Faster Reading

1 Exercise eye movements over page, moving eyes on horizontal and vertical planes diagonally upper left to lower right, and then upper right to lower left. Speed up gradually day by day. Purpose – to train eyes to function more accurately and independently.

2 Read normally for 5 minutes from a book which you will be able to continue using. Record words per minute (w.p.m.).

3 Practise turning 100 pages at approximately 2 seconds per page, moving eyes very rapidly down the page (2 x 2 min. sessions).

4 a Practise as fast as you can for 1 minute, not worrying about comprehension.
   b Read with motivated comprehension – 1 minute.
   c Calculate and record w.p.m.
Repeat as time allows.

5 Use any book (light material) of your choice, preferably one in which you are interested.
Try for as much comprehension as possible, but realise that exercise is concerned primarily with speed. In this exercise reading should continue from the last point reached.
a Practise-read for 1 minute at 100 w.p.m. faster than your highest normal speed
b Practise-read 100 w.p.m. faster than (a).
c Practise-read 100 w.p.m. faster than (b).
d Practise-read 100 w.p.m. faster than (c).
e Practise-read 100 w.p.m. faster than (d).
f Practise-read with comprehension for 1 minute from point reached at end of (e). Calculate and record w.p.m.

6 High Speed Practice 1
a Use any easy book. Start from the beginning of a chapter.
b Practise-read with visual aid, three lines at a time at a *minimum* of 2,000 w.p.m. for 5 minutes.
c Re-read to mark in 4 minutes.
d Re-read to mark in 3 minutes.
e Re-read to mark in 2 minutes.
f Read on from mark, for same comprehension as at (b) for 5 minutes.

7 High Speed Practice 2
a Use any easy book, start at the beginning of a chapter.
b Scan for one minute, using visual aid, 4 seconds per page.
c Practise-read from the beginning at minimum of 2,000 w.p.m. for 5 minutes.
d Repeat this exercise when possible.

paragraphs, from illustrations and diagrams to the footnotes and index), selection and rejection of reading matter, and above all careful study of the conclusion or summary which, with luck, will tell you most of what you want to know about and from the book. This might make 'Inview' unnecessary – for this means careful reading of that material which obviously demands it, and taking notes.

Much as I hate the idea (being a fanatical lover of books as objects) Buzan is clearly right to oppose taking notes while reading. In the first place, it slows you down and may damage overall comprehension. In the second place, you may find yourself taking more and more copious notes than neccssary. So there's no alternative to marking the passages you think to be important; the advice here is to mark softly in the margin with a soft pencil, which I suppose makes the vandalism as limited as possible.

The actual taking of notes, which fits into the Review process, should always be systematic. The choice of system is up to you. But the objective – which is to organize the material, programme it into the computer, and keep it available for reference – will be best served by sticking to a basic method. I always number each page of a notebook and number (or letter) each note. That's because, as a writer, I need to allocate different pieces of material to different sections of a book or article. So I know that 13A, 7B, 16G and so on belong to a particular chapter, and it then becomes simple to refer to the correct note as needed.

If your need is to have a potted guide to a paper, study or book, the sub-division might be better done by subject, following the author's own chapter plan, for an obvious example. But indecipherable, disorganized notes are better than no notes at all for only one reason – the process of comprehension and retention is assisted by translating what is read into what is written. It's an especially powerful form of repetition, since the memory is being attacked, so to speak, from two directions. But the note-taking time is far better spent if, as you zip through the book, jotting down items from the softly marked passages, you are organizing the material into permanently usable form.

Ways of Writing Faster

This doesn't mean using longhand, or long typing. (An advantage of taking notes after, instead of during reading, is that it's easier to use a typewriter.) An average two-fingered typist as I used to be before some self-improvement, at 25 words a minute, is at least 50 per cent faster than a fast legible handwriter. But hand speed can be easily improved by speed-writing – either your own method or somebody else's properly developed system. A simple approach – such as I'm using at this very

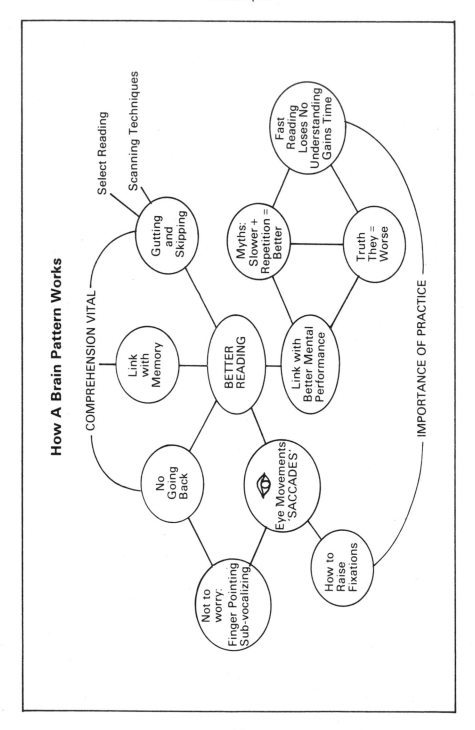

How A Brain Pattern Works

Select Reading

Scanning Techniques

Gutting and Skipping

COMPREHENSION VITAL

Link with Memory

BETTER READING

Link with Better Mental Performance

Myths: Slower + Repetition = Better

Fast Reading Loses No Understanding Gains Time

Truth They = Worse

No Going Back

Eye Movements 'SACCADES'

How to Raise Fixations

Not to worry: Finger Pointing Sub-vocalizing

IMPORTANCE OF PRACTICE

moment – is to have certain standard abbreviations for common words and word endings. A few examples are: the ampersand (&) for 'and', 'tt' for that,
't' for 'the', 'to' and 'it',
'r' for 'are',
's' for 'is'.

In my script, 'v' = very, 'hv'= have, and I always use numerals, not spelt out numbers. The ending 'ing' is always just 'g': 'ed' similarly becomes plain 'd'. The eliminatn of other vowels or endings can easily be mastered (I've just shortened the 'ion' of elimination to a single 'n'). In case you think this all sounds too difficult, see how you manage with the next paragraph.

Xctly t same technqus cn b usd on a typewrtr, whn agn y shld b abl t reduce th time takn by a significnt amount. Initially y wll lose time by stoppg to thnk abt th abbrevtion y'r gng to use. Tt's why t helps to hv set abbrvtns. Go bck to the Bsc Englsh list n the prvs chaptr & rewrte t in speed-hnd. Alwys use the sme abbrvtn, & yr spd wll gn by the full amnt of th lttrs y no lngr use. Whre th shpe of th wrd s unaffctd by th elmntn f vwls, y hv an entrely smple & practcl systm: as I hpe yr undrstndg f ths pssge hs dmnstrtd.

You will need, or at least, benefit from, speed-writing only in traditional note-taking, which I tend to use. That's because of my work: I aim to write an article or chapter to a certain length, and the plan therefore requires a certain number of paragraphs proceeding in a logical, linear order. And it's convenient to have logical, linear notes to slot into the order. But Buzan has achieved remarkable results, sometimes with not very promising human material, by employing the 'brain patterns' mentioned in a previous chapter, which exploit the knowledge that the brain does not, in fact, work in a linear or literary manner.

In other words, the mental process, even though fed by reading books, is not analogous to reading at all. It proceeds by linking key concepts in related groups, just like a brain pattern. On the page opposite you'll find a .pattern on reading, the opening subject of this section. As you can see, it's a freer and easier, more creative, if you like, way of organizing knowledge. Certainly it's worth trying, although, the older you are, the less ready your psyche, as opposed to your brain, may be to accept the concept.

That leaves only one R: Reckoning, which is also a form of reading. Letters and numbers alike are only symbols for realities, and we read figures in the same way as words – though frequently with less comprehension. Some of the same rules apply. For instance, expert adders-up almost always follow the column of numerals with a finger or pointer – you, too, will find that pointing greatly assists addition, except that the ability to add is no longer very useful, because of the calculator. Its electronic capabilities represent a rare example of a machine beating the brain hands (or cells) down. As we noted in an earlier chapter, mechanical calculation is not the brain's forte, any more than it can fix images as conveniently and firmly as a camera. But the calculator – like the slide-rule before it – can be a dangerous weapon. Doing the sums right is important: but doing the right sums in the end matters more. After all, you get nowhere by adding up the wrong column of figures to perfection, and it is in this area of reckoning, of thinking about the real meaning of figures, where traditional education, so strong in mathematics, is relatively weak.

That takes us back to where this chapter on the vital Rs began – with Reasoning, the use of mental power to identify and solve problems. Like associative memory or fast reading, the fast calculation provided by the machine is a tool, a means to an end. The means and the end have to be intelligently chosen by the possessor of all this improved technology, mental and electronic. Only in that way can we hope to achieve the desired end-product: intelligent results.

One last word. This chapter has concentrated on practicalities. But there is magic in words – as, indeed, there is in numbers, for those with the ability, rarer than verbal talent, to master mathematics. The greatest value of an improved reading speed is that marvellous works of literature can be mastered in less time and probably with better understanding. The sovereign grace of memorizing techniques is that the mind retains more of those riches thoroughly. It remains a sad truth that the great bulk of the reading which most people have to absorb in their adult lives is as far from literature as Coca-Cola is from Château Lafite. But if you need to spend less time on the gunk – well, in theory there will be more hours to devote to the glorious. Since these hours, too, will be more productive, it's that happiest of out-turns: an each-way win.

7.
Time and Trouble

THE title of Chapter 2, 'All We Have is Us', could be faulted on one obvious ground: you can argue that all we have is time. The Transactional Analysis school of psychology, as it happens, chooses to regard all human life as an attempt to pass time – or rather to occupy it, since we cannot stop time passing, much as we might wish to. Writing on management, I've observed that the manager's only real resource, personal and even corporate, is time. It is the only expenditure which can't be recouped, since time elapsed is lost for ever.

That being so, the use of time becomes a crucial piece of the manager's equipment – and for anybody who wants to make the best of his life: life being nothing but time. Now, it doesn't follow that the true Superman fills every day, hour and minute of his life with meaningful, organized activity. Good management of time starts from recognizing that idleness, rest, diversion, relaxation are not wastes of time, but constructive and essential uses of the hours.

Waste of time means its employment in useless activities which you intended to be productive, or in inefficient ways – inefficient, that is, in relation to whatever object you are trying to achieve. If you want to organize time, you must know what you want to organize it for, what content you wish the elapsed time to cover, how you will know when the task (i.e. the use of time to achieve your end) has been completed.

In the discussion of reading, I referred briefly to the organization of study – preparing to learn. The organized student, or the organized executive, or the organized housewife, for that matter, first of all decides how much time is available. Then he or she works out how much of the task can be covered in that time: this preliminary job is timetabling or scheduling, and it's well worth the apparently non-productive use of time involved. The more components to the task, the more complex and detailed the timetabling will have to be. Even so, it doesn't normally require much investment of your vital hours.

Contrast this with the disorganized (and unfortunately more

typical) case, who sits down with no idea where or when to start and very possibly finds all manner of distractions and time-wasting to avoid the psychologically unpleasant business of beginning. To start is a barrier. Once surmounted, as part of an organized plan, the start becomes a source of satisfaction. You are off and running – heading on-course towards a known destination.

The extent to which you waste time in ordinary circumstances can be easily tested by keeping a diary (or getting a secretary to keep one for you). Record, over a few weeks, the details of every day, including interruptions, and you will probably be surprised, even horrified, to find how much allegedly productive time is spent unproductively (see pages 94-95).

The wisest writer on such matters – in fact, the sagest sage on any subject to which he has turned his remarkably clear mind – is Peter Drucker, perhaps the only American management expert whose expertise is truly international. Maybe that reflects the fact that he spent the first part of his life (or time) in Europe, and chose in later years to live for a few months in every year in Japan. Which makes it doubly evident that in his own use of time, as a top-level consultant, prolific writer and much sought after lecturer and teacher, Drucker practises what he preaches. That sermon, in turn, is built around the concepts that (1) most senior people don't control more than a quarter of their time; (2) that, the more senior they are, the less of their time they control; and (3) that the self-controlled time is the most important.

As noted, to discover how effectively you use time, you must first analyse it. In most cases the result of an analysis, especially if somebody else does it for the subject, is so distressing that sometimes he refuses to believe the facts. If in your turn you discover that your time is not being spent in anything like the proportions you imagined, remember that the evidence is far more likely to be true than false. There's a great deal to be said, in fact, for keeping a permanent record of your weeks; but the discipline is difficult, and isn't a particularly useful use of somebody else's time. (The President of the United States has a full-time employee who does nothing else but log his master's hours – but the rest of us are less lavishly served at the public expense.)

Questions of Time

Suppose that you do find, as expected, that your time is not well managed. You will want to do something about this very material loss of effectiveness. But what? As we have learnt before, the process of improvement starts from asking questions. Drucker lists three. (1) What am I doing that really does not need to do be done at all – by me or anyone else? (2) Which of the activities on my time-log could be handled

by someone else just as well – if not better? (3) What do I do ⟨
the time of others?

The first two questions run slap into the doctrine of
indispensability. Many of the activities people engage in w ⟨___ ⟩ are
superfluous or disposable (in the sense that they can be transferred to
somebody else) are preserved for reasons of prestige. The time-wasting
routines are thought to go with or enhance the position held. How many
meetings do busy people attend where their presence is really not
required? What evening engagements could be refused without any loss
whatsoever – to host or guest? How many business trips are undertaken
by the boss when some subordinate would be perfectly successful? How
often, come to think of it, is delegation of any kind practised properly?

As Drucker points out, the delegator isn't giving away part of his
personal property – 'my work'. He is merely ensuring that work is
carried out at the most suitable level by the most appropriate person.
That is part of the executive's job, and it doesn't matter whether the
work concerned is professional or voluntary. One object of the exercise,
moreover, must be to free as much time – your own time – as possible.

The objection here is partly puritanical. Ideally, having delegated
efficiently to the right people, the effective time-lord will find himself
sitting with an empty diary at an empty desk. As a matter of observed
fact, the most effective executive I know always does have an empty
desk, and always does have plenty of time to spare – for example, to take
his own phone calls. Now, he may cheat a little by stuffing away in
drawers what might otherwise be on top of his desk, or by taking home
work which, if done in the office, would make him seem much busier.
But even if both these things were true, they would still add up to highly
effective management of time. (On a point of fact, I genuinely believe
that this executive has created abundant time – and in the sense of the
aged Mr Bernstein in *Citizen Kane*, who tells the interviewer: 'I've got
plenty of time. All I've got is time. I'm chairman of the board.')

Wasting the time of other people is a more difficult matter to define.
My own view – in which I am not alone – is that the meeting is the single
greatest abuser of time, followed (quite a distance behind) by the report.
I've often wanted to make it an organizational rule that, whenever two
or three are gathered together for any purpose, stop it: or, two's company,
three is wasting at least one person's time. Of course, I exaggerate. But
it's broadly true that all meetings or committees contain members whose
presence is unnecessary, and that the most efficient way of getting things
done is expressed in the formula one to one to one: that is, one person
given full adequate authority for the task, and both commissioned by
and answerable to one person.

The formula can't be applied in all instances. Often, several
interests, or several areas of expertise, need to be represented in a

Keeping a Time Log

Time	Main Activity	Contact	Rank	Phone
10.27	Budgeting (completed)	AB	sub	
		CD	sec	
		EF	ext	√
		GH	"	√
		IJ	peer	
		CD	sec	
		KL	peer	
		MN	sub	
11.00	Correspondence (completed)	CD	sec	
11.10	Report writing (incomplete)	OP	sub	
		QR	sub	
		IJ	peer	
		CD	sec	
11.30	Studying reports (incomplete)	ST	sub	√
		CD	sec	
12.04	Preparing minutes (completed)	CD	sec	√
		UV	ext	√
		KL	peer	
		OP	sub	√
12.20	External meeting	UV	ext	
12.45	" lunch	YZ	ext	
2.15	(afternoon begins...)			

1 Insert time when main activity changes.
2 Describe main activity and whether completed.
3 Insert name of contact.
4 Give rank (**sub**ordinate, **sec**retary, **ext**ernal, **peer, sup**erior, etc.).
5 Tick if contact is by phone.
6 Or personal call.
7 Tick if the contact was necessary and could not have been put off indefinitely.
8 Tick if the contact was not prearranged or at your request: i.e., tick if it is an interruption.
9 Tick if contact lasts more than 5 minutes.
10 Any comments not covered in first nine columns.

Visit	Essential	Uninvited	Over 5	Note
√	√	√		
√	√			
√	√	√		Private
	√	√	√	
√	√	√		
√	√	√		
√	√			
√				
√	√		√	
√		√		
√	√	√		
√	√	√		Unnecessary check-up
√	√	√		
		√		
√	√	√		
	√	√		
		√		Private
√	√	√		
	√	√	√	Memo possible

In this example, several points stand out. In two hours before he left for an outside meeting, this executive had nineteen contacts, of which fourteen were uninvited: i.e., one interruption every eight minutes. Not surprisingly, two tasks were left unfinished – and five different main activities in less than two hours is too much, anyway. Obviously, he keeps an open door policy: anybody can come in at any time. This may be a virtue in itself, but it has gone too far in this case. The perfect solution, if it's politically possible, is to set aside a period every morning for dealing with all contacts at once. Since only two lasted over five minutes, half an hour would have dealt with most of them. This means that all other contacts should really be screened by his secretary. A more feasible proposition would probably be to invest in a Do Not Disturb sign and tell his secretary he'll return any calls at a given time.

discussion. It follows that somebody should always ask 'Which interests?', and 'Which expertise?' In real life, however, nobody asks; people belong to a given committee because they belong to it, and that's all. The event which precipitated Sir Arnold Weinstock's appointment as managing director of the great General Electric Company in Britain was his refusal to attend any more meetings of the executive committee which was supposed to run the group: Weinstock simply – and rightly – objected to wasting his time on a useless gathering.

As for what happens within meetings, that's another story of time wasted. Yet those attending committees persist in describing the time which is occupied as work – in the same way that many businessmen who spend long hours entertaining other businessmen, usually to large lunches, insist that they, too, are working on these occasions. In the sense that it is time away from home, and paid time at that, it qualifies as work. But in the sense of spending time constructively in achieving personal objectives, or those of the organization, it's a sure thing that nobody has ever 'worked' a sixteen-hour day. These monumental work totals are only achieved by false definitions of work.

The effective use of time thus requires extreme limitation of meetings, for your own sake and those of everybody else; and also the rigorous conduct of meetings, with only enough matters scheduled to fill the allotted time, and with contributions asked for on a pre-planned basis. A meeting isn't a debating society, and can only become a debate if the preparatory work hasn't been properly done. That, too, is the repetition of a golden rule – that the key to becoming an efficient, time-saving executive is careful, intelligent planning.

The initial stages of the Buzan study technique show precisely what this means. First, you decide how long the session is going to be. Second, you decide how much you are going to get through in that period. Third, you go over all the information you already possess on the subject. Fourth, you write down, *as questions,* what you want to obtain from the session. You can see how, although this scheme was devised for study, it translates beautifully into a system for planning a conference – or, indeed, into a general approach to organizing time.

One product of keeping a time-log is the knowledge of how long you do spend in actual work, and how much discretionary time you actually average. Once you have this time framework, you can (after eliminating the unnecessary and the wasteful) place upon the frame the work you want to do. Two basic approaches are helpful. One is to divide the time into units; another is to list the tasks to be completed in a given day – or over longer time periods. It's then a simple matter to marry up the two approaches and arrive at a schedule.

In choosing the the basic time unit, have regard to your personal characteristics and to the nature of your task or work. Remember that work can be carried over: it isn't necessary to complete one task before beginning another. Watch a good cook in a kitchen – which can often be a demonstration of poetry in motion – and you can see how ably and easily the chef switches from one partially finished process to another. But it plainly makes more sense to choose a time unit in which a major portion of a large task, or the whole of a smaller stint, can be accommodated.

Drucker's Practical President

In his *The Effective Executive* Drucker tells a lovely story about the bank president he advised once a month for two years. They discussed only one item at each meeting, and each session lasted exactly one and a half hours. Drucker was always asked to sum up after eighty minutes. The president revealed on questioning that he had 'found that my attention span is about an hour and a half. If I work on any topic longer than this, I begin to repeat myself. But I have also found that nothing of importance can really be tackled in less time.'

Another unusual aspect of this disciplined fellow's interviews was that he was never interrupted, not by the phone, not by his secretary. Why? 'My secretary has strict instructions not to put anyone through except the President of the United States and my wife. The President very rarely calls, and my wife knows better!' After Drucker left, the banker always had an half an hour set aside in which he could answer any calls ('I have yet to come across a crisis which could not wait ninety minutes').

This account has several fascinating aspects, not least of which (for me) is that, over years of retailing the story, I had slowly but unsurely deviated in material aspects from Drucker's original version: which confirms a lesson on memory – that it does need refreshing by reference back. Your time allocation should thus always include periods for revision and reflection, lest you, too, find yourself sliding into error. But note how the banker: (1) fitted the time to his own nature and the necessities; (2) stuck to his timetable; (3) avoided interruptions; and (4) allocated time for the unexpected.

All four are important, but in practice it's often the lack of a buffer zone, time for correspondence, unscheduled interviews, phone calls, etc., that causes pressures to mount intolerably and schedules to run awry. In general, of course, few of us will have the power, even if we have the discipline, to obey the rules as strictly and successfully as the banker. Anybody who tries to edit a newspaper or magazine (which has been a major part of my life for fourteen years) without being disturbed or interrupted is in the wrong line of work. But everybody can move a long way towards the bankerly perfection with only a modicum of effort.

97

The basic time unit will probably revolve around the half-hour. You may require two or three such units (as the banker did to tap the wisdom of Peter Drucker). For other tasks (like catching up on phone calls) one unit will do. In assessing how many units are needed for a task, always over- rather than under-estimate. And always, where possible, leave five minutes in every unit for resting from your labours – as Buzan, for example, recommends after his twenty-five-minute study periods. The purpose is the same as that for the pauses recommended while memorizing – it's to give the computer time to sort out its new load. The break in concentration, while you tidy the desk or wander around the office, will restore, not weaken, your powers.

More – you should schedule 'goofing-off' periods in the day, time when you do nothing except chat, doodle, day-dream. The reasons for this will be referred to again in the chapter on Stress. Here, bear in mind simply that it is unrealistic to ask your mind to concentrate unremittingly on its tasks for every minute of the time available. Because the computer is obedient, it will conform to your directions, but it may well exact a fearful price later on.

Building slack into the day also makes it easier to stick to the timetable, since a slippage or accident can be made up by cutting into the slack time. (That's another virtue of over-estimating and for building slack into the basic time unit – if you haven't quite done as much as you wanted in twenty-five minutes, say, your spare five minutes give you 20 per cent of extra time to exploit.)

Unless you have a special passion for working at all hours, plan your schedule within a normal working day and week. Then the evening and weekend hours can be used as a safety net – preferably only once in a while. The wise person remembers that life and work aren't synonymous, and that the essence of super-management is to use each to reinforce, not destroy, the other. All the means just described will help to provide time for the unexpected, as well as for the expected task that consumes more time even than you have conservatively allotted.

That still leaves the problem of interruptions. In the knowledge that at least four-fifths of all interruptions are unnecessary, you can safely leave the intercom phone off the hook, tell your secretary not to put through any calls, hang a Do Not Disturb sign on the door, and, like our banker friend, deal with any matters arising in the time allotted. The correct approach is to give accurate and clear instructions to any subordinate who might be tempted to break in; with superiors, you are obviously on weaker – even swampy – ground. Striking the right balance is especially difficult because, as we shall see later, remaining approachable is a vital part of man management, and it may conflict (or appear to conflict) with management of time.

Plotting the hours, however, can't end the story. If you can halve the time allocated to your tasks, you can choose (and the choice is especially pleasant) between taking half the time or doing twice as much. Learning to read fast is an obvious example of pouring more result into less time, and the same lesson applies – that, just as a fast reader may understand more (not less), so fast work can be more effective. This apparent contradiction in terms is well known among journalists, who often find that their best work isn't the considered article to which days have been devoted, but the piece rushed out under pressure of a merciless and imminent deadline.

How to Break a Blockage

This particular example may be a virtue created by necessity – false necessity, at that. Journalists are notorious for carrying to extremes the common human fault of procrastination, using every delaying tactic they can think of to avoid actually starting to write. This is the worst kind of time management: an organized writer sets a strict time which leaves an ample stretch for completion and revision. The journalist's block is really an emotional device. Because the writer is frightened of putting words on paper (in case he fails), he creates the external stimulus of a deadline that has come so close that it can no longer be ignored.

That isn't an example to be imitated. The best way to overcome a delaying block – and in delay there lies no plenty, just as the poet Herrick said– is to set a timetable and stick to it: and no matter if the first words you write – or whatever else the task entails –.seem rubbish. A useful preliminary is the ordering of external objects – clearing the desk completely, for instance, except of the material on which you plan to work. But the all-important thing is to start. You may, however, be under pressure which isn't self created: good time management seeks to avoid this, but accidents and emergencies will happen. Their impact, as noted, can be cushioned by leaving slack in your time system, including evenings and weekends; but grace under pressure, or the ability to work faster than normal under time stress, is one of the characteristics that separates the men from the boys, the women from the girls.

This saving grace can be developed by continually searching for ways of speeding up your normal work, so that the habit of acceleration is acquired; or by working under unusual or unfavourable conditions. We've already noted that typing is half as fast again – at least – as longhand, and that speed-typing is faster still. Dictation is faster than either. Careful normal speech, such as you might use for a lecture or broadcast, works out at 160 words a minute. Some people can't even read that fast. Answering memos and letters by writing or typing your reply on the letter received is another time-saver, since it automatically keeps the answer short. Search constantly for short-cuts and use them.

Working in adversity both trains your time-using powers and saves time itself. Waiting for and travelling in planes; sitting in ante-rooms; sitting in conferences during parts that don't interest you; having a quiet lunch by yourself – everybody has fallow time which can be occupied by work. Always carry with you the work materials you will need to take advantage of these periods – paper and pen are obvious, but so are filed papers, clipped articles, accounts. Such periods are also excellent times for planning time – which means carrying with you a memorandum of what tasks lie ahead.

Don't be obsessive about writing time-plans, by the way. Don't plan a day more than once daily, a week more than once a week, a month more than monthly – unless some drastic change demands a wholesale revision. Each list of tasks should be arranged in order of priority. The day's top priority task is the one that you either get out of the way first, or reserve for your best working time, which is something that varies widely from person to person. In most cases, the first working period in the morning is the most productive, and the hours after a large, especially vinous meal are the worst.

The let-down in efficiency should show up quite clearly in your performance of mechanical tasks - in, for example, the greater number of typing errors you will probably make after such a lunch. Fatigue has the same effect, which is why working after a full day at the office, or after a long commute home, is a less good idea than going to bed early, rising early, and starting the task first thing in the morning. Don't fall into the trap of extending the candle at both ends. How long you should work is partly a matter of how long you want to work, true. But there are physical limits to human working potential, and the psychological limits, while they can't be quantified so precisely, exist nonetheless.

The ideal working day or week is the shortest that will accomplish your working objectives – and that goes for your subordinates, too. Forty hours a week is quite enough, maybe more than enough, for any man or woman. Slave drivers who drive themselves don't use time – they abuse it. Subordinates can abuse superiors, too, and not just verbally. Four times out of five, a boss will find that the interruptions in the working day come from below. If interruptions are your problem, it's valuable – in fact, essential – to log them. Once you know where the interruption is coming from you can deal with it. The American time consultant, Alan Lakein, advises making fixed appointments, say, with aides who bob in regularly. This forces them to save up their interruptions for delivery at scheduled times.

You can also (like Peter Drucker's banker) set aside periods when you are not to be interrupted except in very special circumstances: periods which you offset with others when your office door is always open. Lakein warns sensibly that you must ensure that any such arrangement doesn't adversely affect those who work for or with you. When you are interrupted, apply the same test as with correspondence: Is this question/answer really necessary? In the case of correspondence, don't answer when you don't have to answer for now or (sometimes) forever. With interruptions, simply say that you don't want this subject brought to you in future. The object throughout is to reduce the time-load as part of a two-pronged attack on the time period.

The Search for Lost Time

For many busy people, however, the problem is that of never having time for the things you want to do, but which require long hours – like reading *War and Peace*. But this is precisely where time management techniques can help. My equivalent task was reading Proust's *À la recherche du temps perdu*. I set aside a fixed time every day, long enough to cover a fixed number of pages – enough pages to make sense. I could read more pages if I wanted, but never less. My original target was a year. In fact, I finished the great novel in several months less, and the experience of living with the book (which is about the passage of time) through the passage of my own time added an extra and wonderful dimension. In reading, as in work, a little at a time may not be the most efficient approach, but it's better by far than not getting things done at all, and what's more, an excellent method of overcoming a blockage.

The mass of business reading is another aspect of the not-enough-time problem. The load can be eased by flicking through publications, marking the articles which are priority reads, and either clipping them or flagging them (stapling a piece of paper to the relevant pages). You then set aside a period on your schedule for catching up on the unread material, in the knowledge that consuming it doesn't really take much time. The average magazine article won't carry more than 2,500 words. Even at the slow reading speed of 250 w.p.m., that only takes ten minutes. In an hour a week, you can, at a modest reading speed, get through 20,000 words – which is an awful lot of articles.

If all this conjures up a picture of potential total control, forget it. Life and time are not like that. In the first weeks after logging your time, eliminating waste, re-planning the hours, you will achieve vast improvement. Then you will back-slide, quite inevitably. The human computer wasn't designed for controlled 24-hour-a-day operation, and will revert to easier modes as soon as the controller (itself) is looking the other way. But the back-sliding won't be total. Most of the gains will be kept, and you can repeat the time management process again and again. There is thus no reason for back-sliders to berate themselves. Wasting time is part of using time efficiently. You should, after all, be doing what you want to do, and sometimes, quite rightly, that will be nothing at all.

8. The Written and Spoken Word

THERE'S a wonderful moment in *Trilby,* a melodrama remembered today mainly for its villainous impresario Svengali, when the latter peers into the face of his mesmerized soprano victim and exclaims, if I recall correctly, '*Himmel*! The roof of her mouth!' Now, the ability to sing marvellously is indeed a source of wonder, before which lesser mortals can only gape. Other such gifts, inimitable and inexpressible, do exist. But the ability to write well is not among these rarities.

That flat statement doesn't mean that no writer has transcendent ability, still less than anybody can hope to write as well as Evelyn Waugh or as copiously as Harold Robbins. It does mean, however, that the fear and inhibition which attack men and women when they are asked to write is entirely misplaced, and that the strangulated, constipated prose which they produce (which may seem to justify their fears) is the result of those fears, and not of any innate difficulty in the art or any deficiency in themselves.

The analogy is with speaking a foreign language, when lack of confidence, far more than lack of basic knowledge, explains the inability of highly intelligent people to hold a sensible, fluent conversation in French, German, Spanish or some other unfamiliar tongue. Writing shouldn't share the same blockage, since the tongue is familiar: it is the same material which the bad writer uses, mostly with perfect success, in talking to scores of people in an ordinary day. The same literary stumblebum, moreover, may be both fluent and expert using the written word in a personal letter – simply because the psychological barriers involved when writing to a lover or a friend, whatever else they do, don't cause a verbal seizure.

That's why I often advise jittery would-be writers to imagine they are writing a letter home, not composing an article for the newspapers or a report for their superiors. It's true that all literary composition should be adapted to the medium for which it is intended. But no medium demands the faults to which the non-literary writer is prone: the use of

102

long words when short ones will do, choosing passives instead of active verbs, letting sentences ramble on and on, festooning them with capital letters for words that are not proper names, and so on. All the faults, moreover, are elementary – the kind that schoolchildren commit initially and then learn to avoid.

The painful truth is that the bad writer almost certainly expressed himself or herself better in prose at school, partly because of greater practice, partly because of supervision, but more likely because writing essays and themes is a natural activity for the student. So it is for the journalist (though to read the prose of some journalists, you would hardly know it). Writing feels unnatural to the non-writer, and its main defect, not surprisingly, is that it reads unnaturally. Note, for example, how perfectly ordinary people will litter their prose with awful words like 'albeit', 'insomuch', or 'notwithstanding' (words they would never mouth in normal speech), for all the world as if they inhabited the last century.

Write as You Speak

The first rule is to be *natural*. Try to write as you speak. The greatest writers all have this quality of diction: you can almost hear a voice behind the lines, and it is always the same voice. Many writing problems occur simply because the writer is unconsciously parodying somebody else's style. He is writing what he imagines a magazine article or a learned treatise should sound like. Now, parody is about the hardest of all literary arts, which is why so few good examples exist. Small wonder that an amateur trying to imitate a foreign style usually falls flat over his tangled prose. Worse still, the imitative urge becomes infectious, until whole groups of worthies, right across the world, are guilty of the same dreadful insults to language.

In a talk on the B.B.C., John Sparrow, the former Warden of All Souls College, Oxford, gave some perfect examples of contagious literary effluence. Here are two Americans writing about a candidate for an academic job. According to the first, the fellow was 'capable of forming insightful relationships between the elements of his knowledge'. According to the second, the chap was 'sophisticated in interpersonal relationships'. As Sparrow noted, they meant respectively that the candidate could put two and two together and was sensitive about people. Yet both these American academics would have shied away from saying anything so direct – that isn't how university professors are supposed to talk, or rather, write.

Here's an English educationalist, not to be outdone, on the subject of teaching. 'It would be dangerously near to educational abdication to equate a pupil-centred approach with unstructured learning situations.' He seems to be saying, in Sparrow's paraphrase, that 'if you think that taking an interest in the personalities of your pupils involves letting them dictate the syllabus, you might as well give up trying to educate them.' The main criticism of the original passage is not that it is ungainly (which it is), but that it is confusing and unclear. The reader has to stop and think in order to extract a perfectly simple meaning.

Still, it could have been worse. At least there *was* an underlying meaning. Very often, prose becomes convoluted, laden with jargon and obscure because the writer has not clarified his own mind before writing. He chooses to sound clever (by using words and constructions that are wrongly associated with cleverness) because he cannot *be* clever. Our instinct, being modest at heart, is to assume that what we can't understand is too clever for us. Nine times out of ten, if a writer can't express his thoughts in language intelligible to an educated layman, the thoughts weren't worth expressing in the first place.

If you find it hard to accept this truth, consider the case of Alfred North Whitehead, author of a philosophical work called *Adventures of Ideas*. As a youngster I couldn't make head or tail of Whitehead's prose, an inability which I put down to my own intellectual shortcomings. Imagine how delighted I was to read, years later in Bertrand Russell's autobiography, that Whitehead's friend and philosophical partner shared my difficulty completely. Maybe eternal truths of enormous value lurked beneath Whitehead's opaque prose. But since the meaning couldn't be unearthed by anybody else, Whitehead might as well have been spouting gibberish.

Thus, the second stage in writing well is to make up your mind just what it is that you intend to say, and not to succumb to the notion that you can conceal a lack of clarity beneath blankets of bad writing. When the meaning is clear, moreover, compound that virtue by expressing the content in the most direct manner possible. One of the fastest writers I ever met, a man who went on to immense distinction in journalism, was most interested to hear me praising the advice given by George Orwell on the use of direct English. The writer was sure that he personally never infringed the Orwellian rules. So we turned to his article in that morning's paper. Its very first sentence ran: 'It would be less than fair to Mr Gaitskell not to admit. . .'

Just as academics fall into the trap of spouting academic-type verbiage, so do professional writers (like professional talkers) come to rely on devices that allow the typewriter to tick over while the author doesn't actually have to think. If the sentence above, omitting the indirection and the double negative, had said simply 'Mr Gaitskell is right. . .', the thought would have occupied only a third of the space, leaving the writer with considerably more work on hand. Journalists, given the problem of filling space, can be forgiven a particle of their sins; but in general, brevity, in writing, is next to godliness.

Visualizing the Reader

Simplicity isn't very far from divinity, either. The guide is to visualize somebody you know, a person of no expertise in the subject under discussion and no great literary pretensions. If he or she can understand what you're writing, anybody can – and comprehension is what you are trying to achieve. Not only should you visualize an audience: you should form a clear idea of your own literary identity. However, while you should always try to cultivate a natural style and (as advised above) should never strive after artificial effect, since you cannot expect to write in the same vein for wholly different audiences you must know how to adapt.

A journalist quickly becomes a professional chameleon. You cannot write in identical style for the *New Yorker* and *The Times*. Nor should a report to the board be written in the same way as a message to the labour force. In adapting the style to the audience, you necessarily adapt your literary personality. It helps to keep a clear idea of that personality in your own mind. This is a refinement, however, along with such techniques as balancing a sentence, or establishing a prose rhythm, or using repetitions (or avoiding them). Although prose can be refined almost infinitely, à la Flaubert, for most people's purposes Simenon is a far better French model: not only a lucid writer, but a fast one.

One reason for fear of the written task is anxiety about speed, about the time that will be consumed. A previous chapter covered some of the techniques for faster literary performance (see page 87). A basic approach, once you have established your comfortable writing speed, is to measure the task in time units and to stick if at all possible to that timetable. Suppose that you can produce 300 acceptable words in thirty minutes (a reasonable target). Estimate how long your report should be: say, 1,500 words. (As a general rule 1,200 words should be enough for almost anything.) So you have to allow two and a half hours to produce a first draft, on top of any time needed for planning.

Arrange your time accordingly, and allow half as much again for revision. It's far easier to revise on the draft, and get somebody else to do the typing, than to rewrite, because that will take you another two and a half hours. You can now see why Presidents and chairmen need to employ speech-writers. A speech lasting only half an hour will consume 4,800 words. Even a very fast writer, capable of churning out the stuff at twice the rate suggested above, will take four hours to write a draft. No busy executive can easily allow so much of his working day for this purpose – and a Presidential speech will go through several drafts.

The speed of speech, as compared to writing, places a premium on other methods of preparing spoken addresses, which in any event follow different rules from the written word. The basic difference is that a

How to Improve Your Writing

1 Improve your *physical* writing speed.
2 Write as you talk.
3 Plan your writing before you start to write.
4 Use as few words as you need.
5 Avoid circumlocutions, long words when short ones will do, archaicisms, 'it is', passives instead of actives, double negatives, jargon – anything which demands more words and obscures meaning.
6 Make sure that your meaning is absolutely clear.
7 Keep the construction of your sentences simple.
8 Don't revise until you've finished.
9 'Mouth' your words silently to your mind.
10 Preserve a logical, smooth flow.
11 Never strive for effect.

speech generally has to occupy a given time, and a long time at that. A piece of writing will very seldom be as long as 4,800 words, and can usually be as short as the writer wants. Good writing, for all practical purposes, should be as brief as the subject allows – it is an instructive and sometimes humiliating experience to go through a piece of your prose, paring it down as far as possible without weakening the sense. An example is the 87-word précis on good writing on this page. Not only will you save words (and time) by cutting; the style and impact are both likely to be improved. But the speaker, who inevitably eats up words, can rarely afford to lose them – even though, paradoxically, he can afford to say less, in terms of content, than a writer with many fewer words at his disposal.

The explanation is psychological. Tests have shown conclusively that the brain absorbs information through the ear with most difficulty; through the eye with considerably greater ease; and best of all by the combination of eye and ear (audio-visual, if you want the jargon). That explains why TV is so much more powerful a medium than radio:colour TV, too, has more power than black-and-white, because colour has greater visual impact. This means that a speaker who uses multi-coloured audio-visual aids will capture his audience more effectively than an unaided orator (such as the politician on the hustings). The aided speaker will also need less words, since he can pause for his slides and charts to take effect. But he can only reinforce *some* of his 5,000-plus words with pictures: he can't, if he follows convention, project every single word onto a screen.

Thus, the same general limitation applies as to a politician. One such summed up his advice as follows. 'Tell them what you're going to say. Say it. Tell them what you've said. Shut up.' To that must be added Lloyd George's advice to the young Harold Macmillan, who was to follow L.G. to the Premiership many decades later. According to the Welsh wizard, a young Member of Parliament like Macmillan could allow himself one idea in a speech. A Cabinet Minister might be allowed two. A Prime Minister, on important occasions, could get away with three.

Get the People on Your Side

The rules for speeches thus cut right across those for written work. Repetition and word-spinning, often faults on the page, are essential in oratory. If you are confining yourself to three ideas in three-quarters of an hour, you have to go over the ground again and again – and probably again, making four times in all. But a speech, unlike an article or a report, is a performance; and many words will be needed for performing purposes alone. For example, it's wrong to plunge into the heart of the matter. Every speech needs a preamble, a purely introductory section which gives the audience and the speaker time to adjust to each other. This is where jokes come in handy to break the ice, to get the people in the auditorium where they want to be – which is *on your side*.

Public speaking is usually an intimidating experience for the speaker because of the fear that any animal must tend to feel standing at bay confronted by a (potentially) howling pack of (possibly) hyenas and jackals. But the fear cuts both ways. The audience is intimidated by the speaker and wants to please him, which is best done by showing its respectful appreciation. The speaker has to play on this desire to please by attacking the emotions (provoking laughter is the more usual way, but tears will do as well). He can also play on the audience's fear, primarily by fixing it with his glittering eye – which should mostly be aimed at somebody sitting in the centre of the crowd, about a third of the way from the back. The eye can travel, but as with any other gesture, the movement of the eye should be deliberate. Fussy movements, like touching the face, can be converted into forceful gestures, especially if combined with the hardest weapon in the oratorical armoury: the pause. It takes more courage to stand in front of an audience deliberately saying nothing than it does to speak.

Any student of the immortal Jack Benny, the greatest stand-up

107

comic of all time, need look no further for the technique of handling an audience. If the technique is only good enough, the words may escape close attention – which is how Jack Kennedy, for instance, got away with telling his fellow-Americans what was highly unlikely to be true: that they would 'pay any price' in the defence of liberty. But Kennedy's words, even if their sense now seems suspect, could be clearly heard, and audibility is one basic technique which most speakers have to cultivate. (The aforesaid Harold Macmillan was a master of inaudibility when it suited him.)

Clear speech is as valuable off the platform, or the television, as on. The faculty, like athletic ability, reading speed or anything else, can be improved – and in exactly the same way: by practice. Malcolm Morrison, Dean of the School of Drama at North Carolina School of the Arts, has printed, in his excellent *Clear Speech,* several exercises, some of which you will find on the opposite page. Repeating these exercises, whispering first, then speaking, increasing speed without losing clarity, will in itself improve speech quality. But proper speech, as an expert like Morrison will tell you, involves far more than the lips, tongue, and soft palate, which do all the work at the business end. Posture, relaxation and breathing are crucial to good voice production. Morrison thus covers many matters discussed in other chapters in the context of health, stress, and physical fitness. You'll find breathing and relaxation routines in Chapter 13.

But neither will improve your oratory as much as they can - not if you slump, have round shoulders, push the torso forward and upwards (like an army drill sergeant), raise your shoulders towards the ears and push them inwards towards the neck, lean back, push your head in front of the torso, or pull back your head with the chin back against the chest. Any of these posture faults harms your speech. The ideal stance avoids both tension and slumping. Morrison's posture exercises (page 110) are the best I know – and their pay-off is not only in the voice. The physical benefits of standing, and thus walking, properly are great.

A confident, comfortable stance also increases the speaker's moral sway over an audience, even an audience of one. This posture isn't easily maintained if the speaker constantly has to look downwards at a written text. That's why Lyndon Johnson led the fashion for politicos to use a gadget, invisible to the audience, that projects the text at a comfortable height. It serves the same purpose as a tele-prompter for a TV announcer, and the gimmick is much easier and less time-consuming than learning a speech by heart, as Winston Churchill used to do. Politicians, however, are in the unhappy position of having to weigh every word; very few other people need to be so particular. Most can probably afford the luxury of neither preparing a full text nor referring to any text more than occasionally. The trick is to plan your speech by the time to be

Exercising Your Speech Powers

The following jingles and 'tongue-twisters' provide exercise for deft, clear and agile movements of the lips, tongue and soft palate. Follow the routine of whispering, then speaking them. Do not increase speed until you are absolutely sure you can master them at a moderate speed.

1   My organs of articulation,
    Were a definite vexation,
    Until I said this silly rhyme
    Three times through.

2   Many moaning men,
    Making music to the moon,
    Humming down their noses,
    It was a pleasant tune.

3   Writing on a railway train
    Is very hard to do
    For it bumps you up and down
    And shakes you through and through.
    Clickety clack
    Down the track
    Heading for the station,
    I've put my pencil and paper away
    Till I reach my destination.

4   Paul the ape provoked his keeper
    By ripping up banana skins.
    He dropped them in the baboon's cage
    Instead of specially provided bins.
    He pinched peanuts from the people
    Broke his box of plastic plates,
    He pushed big apples through the bars
    And banged and bashed his apey
    mates.

5   Bright blue bubbles,
    Bobby blew and blew,
    Breathing, blowing, breathing,
    Behold. . . .
    Bob became a bubble too!

6   A weasel went walking by the water
    When a worm woke up and said,
    'Will you walk a little quieter,
    I was on my way to bed.'

7   Two dukes tooting
    Two tunes on little flutes,
    'You knew "The Moon in June"
    When we played it on our lutes,'
    Duke One who tooted on the flute
    Was angry with Duke Two, who
    Although he knew 'The Moon in
    June'
    Could not keep his flute in tune
    So he played the lute, instead.

8   Twenty tiny tap dancers
    Tapped to a bright light tune,
    Their routine was smart and dainty
    And they tapped and they did croon.
    Tip tap tappety tap tap tip
    Dippity, dippity tap tap dip.
    Teddy taught the tappers
    To tap and flick their feet,
    But it sometimes happened that the
    twenty
    Tried too hard, and missed a beat,
    So instead of
    Tip tap tappety tap tap tip
    Dippity, dippity, tap tap dip,
    It was
    Tip tappety tappety tip,
    Dippity tappety dip tip dip.

9   A lazy lion lurched along
    A leafy country lane,
    Leaving lots of people
    With a tale too difficult to explain.

These exercises are taken from *Clear Speech* by Malcolm Morrison, published by Pitman, 1977.

109

Exercises to Improve General Posture

1 Stand on the balls of the feet, letting the arms hang loosely by the sides. Gradually lower the heels, keeping the weight slightly forward. Try to retain the feeling of being tall and well balanced as the heels are lowered.
2 Place a finger on top of the head and feel the spine lengthening to push against the finger. The sensation should be that one is growing taller without tension. The head should be well balanced on top of the shoulders, with no feeling of tension round the throat in an attempt to push against the finger. The whole effort of stretching should appear to come from the spine.
3 Bend from the waist, allowing the arms to swing freely, almost touching the floor. Gradually come to a standing position imagining that each of the vertebrae in the spine is placed slowly and carefully one on top of the other, in a vertical position, rather like making a tower with building blocks. The head should be placed on top of the last vertebrae.
4 Deliberately slump, allowing the ribs to sink towards the pelvis and the shoulders to round. Gradually feel yourself growing outwards and upwards as you come to a good standing position feeling taller and wider.
5 Stand against a wall and feel the back of the head and the whole length of the spine contacting the wall. Gradually move away, trying to retain the sense of alignment in the spine and head.

filled – say, thirty minutes. So thirty themes, each expounded for sixty seconds, will accomplish your mission.

The One-Minute Rule

Speaking extempore for a full minute isn't as intimidating as you might suppose – it's only 150 words, which happens to be the length of the previous paragraph. Without looking back, see if you can speak for sixty seconds on the strength of these notes: *"DON'T LOOK DOWN. L.B.J., Churchill, politicians – one point per minute"*. You'll need practice to make perfect, but ten words of notes can easily do the work of 150 complete words. It isn't possible, alas, to compose a 6,000-word speech in a fifteenth of the time: thinking about the subject matter will slow you down, and it's sensible to allow twice the time for preparation that the speech itself will take to deliver. But the value of the method (or any similar one that suits you) lies not only in the time saved, but in the greater natural effect of your speech.

The impact will be all the more if you obey the rules for hearing while speaking. That's to say, remember that the brain's capacity for recalling heard information is low, which is why university students take notes. In most cases, most audiences won't jot anything down, so, if the idea is to leave them with a lasting memory, issue notes yourself – but *after* the speech. It's the reverse of the rule for gestures. Another piece of advice, this time from Harold Macmillan, is to make the gesture first: the raised fist, the Kennedy chop, or whatever. Then, having arrested the audience's attention, you deliver the punch line. Notes distributed beforehand, however, may dilute your impact. Delivered after, they will enable the audience to overcome the typical problem: while impressed by what the speaker said, they are quite unable to recall a single word.

In your own capacity as listener, do record whatever you feel is worth remembering – but do it quickly. You, too, could train your mind, as Truman Capote did, to work like a perfect tape recorder. But this isn't a skill most people need, and, however well developed your verbal recall, it deteriorates rapidly, like an ancient wine once opened. Try writing down a conversation shortly afterwards, and it's amazing how much you can remember – just as a dream unfolds in its seeming entirety if you write it down immediately on waking. A day later, however, and little will remain except the name of the other party.

Unlike brilliant writing, or spell-binding oratory, good recall is a matter of straightforward practice. But writing and speaking, too, improve greatly, if not to the level of brilliance, with repetition and with the abolition of fear. The fear is futile. Everybody finds it easy to communicate something in clear written or spoken language to somebody. If the trick can be managed once, it can be achieved always – and by anybody.

9.
Do Unto Others

CONSIDERING that human beings have been relating to each other for thousands of years, the boom in the inter-personal industry is one of the oddest phenomena of our times. The insights of Sigmund Freud are probably responsible, as they are for so many other fashions – and so many real human advances. Freud taught man to confront and to conquer (or try to) the demons that lurked within. It was only a short step (though it took several decades) to recognition that the demons within played havoc without - as the respective possessors or possessed of the demons confronted each other and tried to achieve some kind of intercourse.

Particular inter-personal theories may or may not be true; but their practice has had phenomenal success. It's not surprising. Very few people are truly confident about their relationships with other people, except a few especially close loved ones, and sometimes not even them. Even hard-boiled managers can easily be persuaded that they don't know how to handle other people, or that others 'perceive' them (that's a great inter-personal word, perceive) quite differently and more un-favourably than they themselves suppose. If you can cure a damaged psyche, then, surely, you can cure a failure to relate to others – can't you?

The sad message of this chapter is that you probably can't, not that easily. Having problems with other people is no sin; if it is, all the world are sinners. And this is one field where self-development has strict limitations. To relate to other people you need another person – and you cannot develop them, or control their behaviour, to suit your needs. That is one of the many weaknesses of the various kinds of encounter therapy that first burst into the media with the Esalen Institute (whose founder, Dr Patrick Murphy, is now - or was, at the last report - into physical fitness as the ultimate in spiritual liberation) and have reached some kind of apotheosis with E.S.T.

In all these experiences, which may be very enriching, or very disturbing, the subject is mixing with like subjects, by definition. Everybody is there to stroke and be stroked, and to expose their tender egos for a dose of bruising. Even if the exposure assists in relating to these people (who may, of course, include your ever-loving spouse), that isn't necessarily going to help with non-members of the group – i.e., almost everybody else in the world. Anyway, are you really sure that the inhibitions built up over ages of social evolution are unhealthy, or, more important, that your own problems do actually result from fear of touching and being touched, say?

The ethological guru Dr Desmond Morris is greatly impressed by the lengths to which people go to avoid bumping into each other in the street; not only that, but we apologize profusely if by some unhappy chance we do make physical contact in this way. Aha! – to a guru, or at any rate to this guru, it all means that we have been conditioned to avoid touching each other. The more obvious point is simply ignored. If you knock into somebody accidentally, it's liable to hurt. We don't avoid treading on people's toes, or having our own stamped on, because of some artificial fear bred into us in childhood. We avoid it because it hurts; and, if we hurt other people, they might hurt us back.

The rules of social behaviour all have similar sound foundations. We shake hands with the right to prove that we're not about to stab the other guy with our trusty poignard. The idea is archaic, but you can see that it was eminently practical. Good manners between men and women mostly derive from sexual courtship. Part of the Western male's role, back as far as the Stone Age, is to protect the female. So men in the West walk on the ouside of the pavement, lest their lady get splashed with the mud from a passing carriage. It isn't quite the same thing as slaying a marauding mastodon – but it is, to use a beloved modern phrase, a piece of role-playing.

Eric Berne's Gripping Insight

The fact that we play roles, or games, in inter-personal relationships was brilliantly exploited by the late Eric Berne in *Games People Play*. (There must be some explanation, though I can't imagine what, for the odd fact that the guru of Transactional Analysis, Berne, and the guru of the media, Marshall McLuhan, both emerged from Canada.) Berne's work, completely disregarded when it made its first appearance, but a world best seller the second time round, was exploited in its turn by *I'm OK – You're OK* – Thomas Harris and a whole school of followers. It's a gripping insight, too: the thought that from our relationship with our parents and from the formation of the child, parent and adult patterns in ourselves, we derive four basic concepts about existence.

(1) I'm Not OK, You're OK
(2) I'm Not OK, You're Not OK
(3) I'm OK, You're Not OK
(4) I'm OK, You're OK (the ideal condition)

There's a marvellous story about how the great screen writer Herman Mankiewicz lost his job at Columbia. The czar of the studio, the horrific Harry Cohn, was telling the lunch table how he knew whether a picture would be box office or not: if his fanny twitched in the viewing room chair, no go. Mank did himself in with the loud remark, 'Gee, think of it – the whole world wired to Harry Cohn's ass.' Well – Gee, think of it – all human relationships reduced to four postulates! The OK/Not OK formulations may help you to get your bearings in certain situations, or even to understand yourself a little better, maybe a lot better. They are certainly a valuable guide to your personal conduct in exchanges with others (see p. 116-7). But they are no no panacea – because, in the matter of relations with others, there are no panaceas.

Such relations, for a start, fall into several sharply varied categories. The first group, rightly first because it comes first in the process of life itself, is Intimate. That in turn breaks down into the Hereditary (close family) and the Acquired (lovers, spouses and close friends). At the opposite extreme is the Casual – people whom you may meet only once, across a shop counter, say; or they could be met many times without either party ever stepping outside the bounds of the particular transaction that produced the contact in the first place. In between the two extremes fall a whole host of gradations in three main sub-divisions: Social, Working and Functional.

Only the last needs explanation. It is an expansion of the Casual – the relationship, for example, with a gardener, a golf pro, a secretary, a butcher, a connection which has its basis in the functional need that brings two or more people together, but which becomes more than that, a friendship without intimacy.

Most people feel and behave quite differently about these several categories of relationship, as you would only expect. The extremes of irrational behaviour are found at the extremes. Husbands will talk to wives, and vice versa, in tones and terms of vituperation which they would never use to anybody else – except, possibly, some total stranger who obstructs their car with his own. On the road, as in the home, something akin to madness may take over. If a travel delay is involved, it will probably be insignificant. Even if the cars have actually collided, flying into a raving fury will accomplish nothing.

There are other cases of lunatic behaviour by evidently sane people. The office thug is a case in point. His megalomaniacal conduct is often not repeated at home, so it can't be attributed to some generalized mental disorder. At work he is an acute example of continuous aggressive behaviour of the type which most men and women employ only rarely. The scientific evidence purporting to show that man is an uniquely aggressive animal is no more convincing than the historical evidence. Most of the soldiers engaged in and killed by wars (especially in this century) have been extremely reluctant fighters. But everybody at some time or another shows aggressive behaviour. Why?

The Cop and the Driver

The important new insight provided by the ethologists encapsulates the truth in an old French saying: '*Cet animal est méchant. Quand on l'attaque, il se défend.*' The aggressor in the animal kingdom is usually defending his vital interests, growling or lashing out to prevent encroachments on his own territory. Human animals are no different.

One of the really useful hints to emerge from ethological research was the right technique for dealing with a cop who stops your speeding or otherwise delinquent car. Don't, runs the advice, stay in the vehicle. The cop perceives the car as *your* territory, and gets on the defensive because of your implicit aggression in not surrendering that territory. Get out of the car, and you've made a submissive gesture – which may save you a ticket, if you're lucky. The theory would explain people's strange belligerence in cars. Since the car is our portable territory, the man who blocks our progress is interfering with primal urges of possession and occupation. We are all bundles of atavistic emotions, in fact, and these attitudes come bursting out in the two situations where we are under least restraint by civilized convention: in intimate relationships of the husband/wife, parent/child variety, and those remote, accidental contacts in which we are not compelled to recognize the other person as a human being at all.

Hence the quite common turnabout when one man (or woman) starts to blast hell out of another driver, only to stop dead, even turn to smiles, when the villain is revealed as a friend or acquaintance. The offence, imagined or real, is the same. But the attitude is entirely different. The primitive aggression gets overlaid by the civilised constraints, just as the aggression itself may subside into submissive fear if the other driver proves to be a more aggressive and powerful animal than yourself.

OK: so you're atavistic, a throwback to early man. What are you going to do about it? The first question to answer is whether your attitude to other people and ability to relate to them are actually causing you any pain, trouble or disadvantage. If not, there is no need to bother. You may be horrible, but you work. And in the great majority of cases

115

How to Conduct Transactions

1   Recognize the Child in yourself, its vulnerabilities, its fears, its principal methods of expressing these feelings, *its worry about being not OK.*
    Q: *Am I being childish?*

2   Recognize the Parent in yourself, its admonitions, injunctions, fixed positions and principal ways of expressing those admonitions, positions and injunctions.
    Q: *Am I reverting to my parental archetypes?*

3   Be sensitive to the Child in others, talk to that Child, stroke that Child, protect that Child, appreciate its need for creative expression, as well as the Not OK burden it carries around.
    Q: *Am I being as sympathetic towards this person as I would hope to be towards my own child?*

4   Count to ten, if necessary, in order to give the Adult time to process the data coming into the computer, and to sort out Parent and Child from reality.
    Q: *Have I properly understood the situation?*

5   When in doubt, leave it out. You can't be attacked for what you didn't say.
    Q: *Do I really need to say/do this?*

6   Work out a system of values. *In fact, one such system is implicit in these instructions and questions.*
    Q: *What system of values does this approach imply?*
    A: *The recognition that other people's sensitivities and problems are as important as your own.*

These tables are based on *I'm OK — You're OK* by Thomas A. Harris, published by Jonathan Cape, 1973. The passages in ordinary type are reprinted by permission of the publisher. Italicized passages are by the author.

Recognize the Parent by:

1 Furrowed brow.
2 Pursed lips.
3 Pointing index finger.
4 Head-wagging.
5 The 'horrified look'.
6 Foot tapping
7 Hands on hips.
8 Arms folded across chest.
9 Wringing hands.
10 Tongue-clicking.
11 Sighing.
12 Patting others on head.
13 'I'm going to stop this once and for all.'
14 'I can't for the life of me'.
15 'Always'.
16 'Never'.
17 'How many times have I told you'.
18 'If I were you'.
19 'How dare you'.
20 'Naughty', 'stupid', 'ridiculous', 'disgusting', etc.
21 'Sorry', 'honey', 'poor dear', etc.
22 'Now what?'
23 'Not again?'

Recognize the Child by:

1 Tears.
2 Quivering lips.
3 Pouting.
4 Temper tantrums.
5 High-pitched whining voice.
6 Rolling eyes.
7 Shrugging shoulders.
8 Downcast eyes.
9 Teasing.
10 Delight.
11 Laughter.
12 Hand-raising for permission to speak.
13 Nail-biting.
14 Nose-thumbing.
15 Squirming.
16 Giggling
17 'I wish' and 'I want'.
18 'I don't know' and 'I don't care'.
19 'I guess'.
20 'Bigger, biggest, better, best'.

By recognizing the Child and the Parent in yourself you can adjust your behaviour to the Adult role. By recognizing the behaviour pattern of others, you can adjust your own accordingly.

and relationships, outside the two extreme categories (the Intimate one in particular), most people do work reasonably well – certainly well enough to cope.

If you cannot cope, you need help. But if you are looking for a basic character change in six easy lessons, or sixty, forget it. That isn't how the super-computer works. At a conscious level, behaviour can be modified in many ways: some re-programming can be achieved by techniques such as those described in this book. They will not, however, produce a changed, born-again man or woman. The fashionable bundles of techniques sold today to seekers after better personal relationships will definitely provide assistance in obtaining greater self-control (which includes 'uncontrol', the ability to let your hair down at the right time). The effects of such lessons can be lasting. But emotional control, more than any other form of taking thought, is subject to the law of diminishing returns.

To take an easy example, who could fail to be moved by the testimony of a lady, a lifelong friend of Mozart's, printed as an epilogue to his collected letters, that 'All my life, I have never seen Mozart in a temper, still less, angry'? It's easy enough, encouraged by that noble example, to discipline yourself for quite a few days into a condition of total calm and unreasonable sweetness. The attitude makes life a great deal more pleasant, too. But before long something or somebody is sure to 'make you angry'.

The phrase, like most common speech, is instructive. You are 'made' angry, as if the compelling force were outside the self. That's what angry people would like to believe. The truth is that the force is inside them, but that it might as well be outside for all they can do about it. Not so incidentally, if it's any consolation, the lady was wrong (she was writing 34 years after his death). Mozart's letters themselves reveal that he was frequently livid with all manner of people, especially patrons and rival musicians.

Anyway, as the encounter therapists stress, it's good to let all your emotions out, including the rabid ones, like violent irritation. While the wrongs of repression can be greatly exaggerated, emotional constipation is not to be recommended. Yet, however much self-control and uncontrol you are able to deploy, that can never solve all your people-to-people problems, simply because you cannot be sure that others will be equally controlled, or that their desires and objectives will coincide with yours. Conflicts and tensions will still arise at the points where personalities and personal interests collide. The best you can do is to know what your own purposes are. Even if they are fatally obstructed by others, at least your own tactics and strategy can be mapped out in accordance with an intelligent master-plan.

The Ghost v the Beast

It's the old conflict between the Ghost and the Beast described in Chapter 5. The Beast, when attacked or fearing attack, wants to fight. The Ghost, if the forces of reason are allowed to operate, may well see no purpose in staging a stand-up row. Suppose that an argument does develop. If the outcome is fundamentally unimportant to you, then it doesn't (again fundamentally) matter whether you win or not – except that you may be one of those many unfortunates to whom power and victory matter at all times for their own sakes. Such people are not interested in the substance of the argument, but in the argument itself.

This was one of the fatal character weaknesses of the former British Prime Minister Edward Heath. He appeared to think that to compromise was to show weakness: better to be strong and wrong than weak and right. It's true that largely irrational ideas of force and power do sometimes play a crucial role in the conduct of human affairs. But they can hardly play a useful part unless the causes to which they are harnessed are the right causes; and right can't be established by might, whatever the dead and defeated dictators believed on the subject. It is nearly always wrong to assert authority for its own sake, or to refuse to take some action 'on principle'.

Not that authority doesn't sometimes have to be defended, or that people shouldn't have principles. But the principles on which men and women usually make their stands are rarely those of the ethical type (most of which are neatly and admirably covered by the Biblical maxim, 'do unto others as you would be done by'). 'Principle' is generally a euphemism for pride and prejudice. If you are being asked to commit a crime, or to damage another human being wantonly, the answer is clear: No. But if the question is whether to take a holiday in Italy or Sussex, no good 'principle' is served by insisting on taking the decision yourself. And that is just as true if the issue is the appointment of a new marketing director.

In business or professional situations, it shouldn't be difficult to solve the two basic problems: What do I want, and who am I, anyway? The job and the role are normally given, and you only need to establish a clear enough identity to perform your part to an acceptable standard (acceptable to other people, even if it isn't to you). Difficulties with relationships shouldn't loom large in the working life: or certainly no larger than the questions of effective use of time, mental powers and the physical faculties which were discussed in earlier chapters. It could be that you're in a highly charged political climate to which this whole paragraph doesn't apply, and which makes the worst domestic hurly-burly seem a haven of peace and quiet. But unless you are among the

119

personality types who crave conflict and conniving, the solution, if at all possible, is to escape – and quickly.

You *can* run away from trouble, and there's nothing wrong or shameful in doing so. 'Anything for an easy life' is regarded commonly as a piece of moral lassitude: just as the man who says 'I could have taken the easy way out' thinks himself, and is thought to be, some kind of moral hero. As the British journalist Samuel Brittan once noted, only a fool takes the hard route when an easier one is available. The ideal way of controlling personal relationships is the same as the best method of using your time: to accomplish what has to be done as efficiently as you can with the least possible use of resources – and emotions are certainly among your vital reserves.

So is the ability to persuade, influence or even dominate others. Again, these talents make little sense in a vacuum. Nobody gets any prizes for persuading a group into some course of entirely futile action about which the persuader doesn't care himself. The much-maligned Machiavelli has provided more useful advice than anybody else on how to impose your will on others; but that wise Florentine would never have dreamt of advising a prince to pursue a worthless or unclear objective. It's by no means immoral, however, to use the Machiavellian approach to achieve a chosen end. In today's society, when compulsion has become increasingly hard to apply, even in authoritarian and hierarchic organizations like the Church and the Army, Machiavellian, or at any rate, manipulative methods may be essential.

Mothers have long known how to make children finish their lunch by distracting their attention with a story. We all have little ploys to help win games and friends, to influence people and events. Inside a modern business, the executive in charge may be as sure of his decision as any nineteenth-century industrial autocrat. But to get his way, today's man may have to cajole a workforce which in the past could have been commanded; he may even have to persuade them into believing that his own idea is actually theirs – a truly Machiavellian feat.

The technique of getting your own way by giving others the false impression that it is *their* own way has been practised since time immemorial in the opposite direction – that is, by the subordinate outwitting (you might say) his boss. Wives are adept at employing the same ruse on husbands. In a sense, it involves duplicity (which is why Machiavelli has such a bad name): the protagonist does not come clean, he conceals his true intentions, he does not share all the available information, he keeps cards up his sleeve. In other words, his behaviour is in flat contradiction to the openness, the let-it-all-hang-out honesty preached by the encounter therapists, and by the apostles of better industrial communication and consultation (both stem from the same behavioural science schools).

The Communications Multiple

The two contradictory approaches would be reconciled if people in the mass could be relied upon to behave even as sensibly as individuals. But often the opposite is true. Take any group of ten people individually and discuss a contentious issue: a goodly proportion will adopt reasonable attitudes. Take the same ten, and have the issue discussed collectively, and mayhem may result. The probable reason is that where the one-to-one relationship (which, heaven knows, can be difficult enough) has only two communication channels (me to you and you to me) a three-way communication has six such channels, and the number goes on rising geometrically into astronomical zones.

All communication is bedevilled by the fact that what the communicator says may not even accurately express what he thinks or wants to say, while what the listener hears may not accurately reflect either. A simple, casual commendation, like 'That's a great job you've done there, Jack', may give rise to an anxious reaction, like 'Why's he saying that to me?' (But don't let that example put you off using praise as an inter-personal tool; it can be just as effective as the whip, and is much easier to use: flattery will always get you somewhere.) Multiply the number of communicants and communications, and it's small wonder that misunderstandings abound. Moreover, since the incomprehension is irrational (if the protagonist is being reasonable himself), you're right back in the same mess as a female confronted by a ranting male, or the other way round: reason won't solve the problem, no matter how hard you try.

The difference is that while the domestic crisis may never be solved, short of divorce, collective troubles within any organization, voluntary or otherwise, generally are solved. The workers on strike against a company have a vested interest in that company's survival. If it doesn't continue, they can't receive the higher wages they seek. At that point, their interests and the company's coincide, so that a settlement, however long it takes, is inevitable. It may take a confrontation, like the strike, which is a wasteful procedure, to bring about the settlement. But failure to use reason always involves waste, and confrontation is sometimes inevitable - even though it is something which most humans most of the time positively dislike.

The dislike is painfully evident in a quite common one-to-one encounter: when a subordinate must be fired. Captains of industry with a reputation for total ruthlessness have been known to quail before this task. Yet the position of the boss could hardly be more dominant: the man about to be fired is rarely in any position to challenge the decision, his psychological defences are likely to be shattered, he won't (in all probability) try to sock his boss on the jaw, he is even unlikely to weep (the classic feminine offensive-defensive ploy in a domestic conflict). So what explains this fear of firing?

It can't be humanitarian dislike of inflicting pain on another person, because the original decision to fire, taken in the absence of the victim, usually causes much less trouble. Any experienced executive knows that keeping on an employee who can't do the job is bad for both the organization and the man; that the latter, more often than not, is fully aware of his failure and may even, in a deep psychological sense, long for the blow to fall; and that many dismissed people end up in far better and more suitable jobs than the one they have lost. Any housewife knows, too, that no good purpose is served by employing a cleaning lady who doesn't clean, or a laundry that doesn't launder. The decisions that must be executed are axiomatic.

The explanation of reluctance to face the firing interview can only lie in the complex of emotions at the core of the person who must do the firing. Maybe it is self-identification that hurts most: the firer puts himself in the victim's shoes, quite involuntarily. But whatever the cause or causes, the result is irrational fear, the creation of a paradoxical false insecurity in the mind of the man who is actually undermining the security of somebody else, and has a licence to do so. Like all irrational fears, from that of the dark to that of making a public speech, this one can be overcome by the simple act of doing that of which you are afraid. Confront a fear head-on, and in all save the extreme cases it will diminish: carry on confronting, and the fear will eventually dwindle into less than a memory.

Yet the fact that firing and other disciplinary confrontations arouse fear is not unhealthy. British headmasters who hated to spare the rod were traditionally fond of saying, as they spared it not, 'This hurts me more than it hurts you.' It would have been better for the victims, and for the floggers themselves, if this sanctimonious nonsense had been true. Like flinching from fire, the automatic reflex which prevents severe burns, shying away from hurting other people is a mutually protective mechanism, one of the psychological forces that help to make relationships between human beings tolerable. The atavistic Beast in the Machine isn't only destructive by any means. His objectives include in overwhelming degree self-preservation, which in turn demands the preservation of others (If I don't hurt you, you won't hurt me; you scratch my back, I'll scratch yours).

Like fears, these other inner forces are better managed if they are identified and confronted, which is one real contribution which psychotherapy and group therapies can make. Coming as near as you can to knowledge of the self should be part of the object of life, anyway. Beware only of the fact that all such knowledge is subjective in both formation and interpretation. Arthur Koestler has reported that one Swiss professor of psychology used to make all his pupils submit a sample of their handwriting, to be sent to a leading graphologist; they were then all given a copy of his assessment of their personalities, which they all found amazingly perceptive; the wily (or Machiavellian) professor then revealed that he had given them all exactly the same assessment.

You can apply the same test yourself by reading horoscopes for somebody else's birthdate. It is likely to read just as convincingly as your own. This isn't only because astrologers, like fortune-tellers, are professionally expert at producing communications that will mean what the listener wants them to mean. The more important difficulty is that everybody contains conflicting characteristics, and that the subjective adjectives which describe these traits are themselves vague. Are you generous or mean? Weak or strong? Idealistic or materialistic?

Sometimes you're one, sometimes the other. Or you may be both all the time. It depends (to use that favourite inter-personal word once more) on how you perceive yourself and are perceived by others. But it's no use crying over that spilt milk. The perception which you must attempt to clarify is that of the objectives which you wish to achieve as a result of your personal relationships, face-to-face or in a crowd. Much of the time you will fail. But the better you are managed yourself, the better you will be able to manage others – to your mutual benefit.

10.
The Bitch Goddess

CALL no man successful until he's dead. In obituaries, men and women seldom fail. In real life they fail frequently, and the more successful they appear to the outside world, the greater their skill and achievement in their chosen field, the more likely they often are to depreciate their success and to agonize over their shortcomings. The political cartoonist Vicky, who succeeded to the post in the *Evening Standard* held by the great David Low, and excelled him, decided inexplicably at the height of his powers that the latter were declining, and committed suicide. It was an extreme case. But creative genius is rarely satisfied with its creations, because success to a creator is measured by the distance between what he had in mind and what he has actually produced.

Only the mediocre artist is satisfied by the applause of the crowd – though applause is a highly acceptable currency of success. The occupations which attract applause (like performing music, the theatre, sport) thus have a head start in the gratification stakes over solitary pursuits like writing or business management, where plaudits come in individual instalments (if at all) and not in the form of a crowded auditorium of people rising to their feet and clapping their hands sore.

This truth shows one of the essential ingredients of success: the reaction of others. The more favourably they react, the greater, on this dimension, success will be. The rare case is indifferent to public or critical opinion – like Gustav Mahler, who was convinced (rightly, as it turned out) that his symphonies were written for the appreciation of listeners fifty years after his time. But Mahler was no failure. He was one of the most admired and sought-after conductors of his time, and no stranger to tumultuous applause. So this exception by no means disproves the rule, which is that success to a large extent is measured by what the world calls successful.

Money is a good example. Nobody would dream of calling a rich man a failure (oddly enough, even if the wealth is inherited). A millionaire is by definition a very successful person, even though, as I pointed out in *The Common Millionaire,* published in 1974, a millionaire in the early seventies was worth only £117,000 in 1914 money, and only £378,000 in the currency of 1948. Yet the modern millionaire isn't regarded as any less successful (though on the money measure he certainly is) than his predecessors. In the popular mind, a million equals success, and always will, until inflation reduces it to a sum within the reach of the ordinary, unsuccessful man.

But is a man necessarily unsuccessful because he isn't rich, or a success because he is wealthy? The answer to the first question is obviously no, since a multitude of successful activities have little or no direct monetary reward attached – winning academic laurel wreaths, running the marathon, deciphering the Minoan script known as Linear B, and so on, and on, and on. Wealthy failures are also common: men who have lost positions of power, or failed to realize long-held ambitions – lesser versions of William Randolph Hearst, declining in his grotesque castle amid the debris of his hopes.

Still, it's a convenient myth, treasured by the rest of us, that rich men are all miserable. Don't you believe it. Wealth is a very comforting possession, though its comforts are by no means as considerable as, at the other end of the scale, the pains of poverty are harsh. Material comfort (which means as much of the world's material goods and services as you happen to want) is a perfectly legitimate target: and those who are successful on other measures tend to gripe bitterly if they lack enough monetary reward to buy the cars or other goodies that their less successful neighbours enjoy.

A well known phenomenon of money, however, is that the desired salary level is always one or two stages above the actual pay. That is, a man on £5,000 a year will think £6,000 or £7,000 to be riches indeed: arrived at the next stage, he rapidly concludes that £8,000 or £9,000 is the earthly paradise. Money is an essential ingredient of success for most people in most circumstances, and it's silly to pretend that it isn't. Yet some people do pretend, mainly because money troubles most people, whether they consider themselves successful or not; why this is so will be covered in Chapter 12. But the key word in the last sentence is 'consider'. The adequacy or inadequacy of income, above a certain minimum level of subsistence and social standards, is in the mind of the possessor (and to a certain extent that of the beholder). The owner of the income will feel happier about its size if he knows that others regard the amount with a nice, comforting degree, not of envy necessarily, but admiration.

Every Flea Has A Bigger Flea

The admiration or jealousy of others may be a comfort. But your own jealousy destroys the peace of mind which success, or the feeling of success, should bring. Talk to one successful playwright (whose plays invariably get produced, always win wonderful reviews, usually get filmed), and you will find that he envies the success of another writer. Talk to the latter and he will be jealous of still another man of the theatre. It seems that every flea has a bigger flea upon his back to bug him. Like all emotions, this one is impervious to reason. The competitive drive is part of the equipment required for success in most fields, and it implies ranking yourself in comparison with others – however irrational this might be.

It makes sense in some contexts. For instance, if you are an athlete, or an ocean racer, or a chess player – in other words, involved in any activity where you have opponents and a clear means of distinguishing between success and failure – you have no option but to compare yourself with others. At the highest level, however, does another Olympic finalist feel jealous of the gold medal winner, in the same sense that a senior executive envies a colleague who has been promoted to the board? Anybody who is a true professional, in the sense of a dedicated and highly trained practitioner of the art, sport or craft concerned, is as deeply interested in absolute performance as in the relativities. Perfectionism needn't mean victory.

The top athlete, in effect, is always competing primarily with himself: fighting against his own resistance to achieving the highest standards. Exactly the same is true of any serious practitioner of any form of human activity. Note that success, judged along these lines, lies in the degree of satisfaction which the performer gets from his or her performance. Athletic coaches at schools make a profound mistake when they force children to judge their running, say, by the position they achieve in races. The coaches only turn into a disagreeable experience what could be a source of lifetime pleasure.

A slow runner can enjoy his run just as deeply as a track star: probably more, since the star will be striving harder for a goal that is always tantalizingly out of reach. The sense of achievement (or success) in running your first sub-ten-minute mile is not reduced, if you started at 12 minutes, by the knowledge that you are still a tortoise compared to the athletic hares. Success in this inner sense means setting objectives which are worth reaching and which are within reach, and then attaining that goal. The manner of performance, too, can build the sense of achievement: to do with ease and grace that which you've never achieved before is sublime, even if the absolute level of performance is still ridiculous.

For lucky people, inner success may be enough. The process of setting and attaining ambitions can be endless, with each stage replaced by another, either in the same field or some new venture. After you have finally read *War and Peace,* you can switch to mastering colloquial German, and then move on to the art of French cooking. Or you may be perfectly content to repeat the activities you have mastered (mastered in the sense of doing them as well as you want). Inevitably, as the learning curve operates, performance will improve. The improvement isn't necessary to confirm this internal and indispensable achievement of success, but any career plan should allow time for the curve to take effect – and should also allow for its beneficial impact on further progress.

The bitch goddess won't be fobbed off by a knowledge of silver hallmarks or the best vintages of Burgundy since 1945. Those who have ambition must move out of the inner world into the external one. Inevitably, success will be measured by them, and by others, on the scale of recognition. Here the first difficulty is that objectives are much harder to fix. It is possible to make some of them as precise as the mastering of French irregular verbs or the running of a seven-minute mile. With money, for instance, career goals can always be set in terms of so much income, so much capital. Doing so has another virtue, in that it provides a basis for financial budgeting.

Precise goals in terms of goods (which are the same as money, since the latter can be translated into possessions) are also feasible. Somehow, it's more enticing to have the ambition of owning a three-bedroomed villa in Provence by the age of 35 than to think in terms of its financial equivalent. Material aims have the disadvantage that most of us, by definition, will find other people with more evident 'success': also, the realized ambition tends to lose its charm with familiarity. The three-bedroomed villa begins to look too cramped, maybe: just as the £10,000 salary, once enjoyed, begins to seem no more than barely adequate.

Yet the achievement of a formulated ambition is probably more satisfying than achievement undirected. 'I've got where I wanted to' is an enormously reassuring statement. And naming a destination in non-material terms is perfectly sensible, whatever the difficulties. If you want to be chief executive of a major public company by the age of 40, or a Cabinet member by 45, or a best-selling author by 50 – then, provided that you have the necessary qualities, these are reasonable ambitions from which rational courses of action can be deduced. Success cannot be commanded – especially in the form of public recognition. But it can always be planned.

Trivial Many, Vital Few

Part of the plan should be to concentrate effort where it will do most good. No law of human behaviour has been confirmed so conclusively and in so many different contexts as the law of the trivial many and the vital few – first propounded by the Italian economist Pareto. To be precise, 'In any series of elements to be controlled, a selected small fraction in terms of numbers of elements almost always accounts for a large fraction in terms of effort'. What this means for you is that finding the small fraction (usually around 20 per cent) and concentrating 80 per cent of your effort on that (because that is where 80 per cent of the problem or the achievement lies) is a sure guide to better performance.

To illustrate, Pareto's law means that a fifth of the customers nearly always provide four-fifths of the turnover, a fifth of the product range represents four-fifths of the sales, a few of the people in a department do most of the effective work. The law helps by (a) defining the areas where your efforts can achieve greatest performance and thus success; and (b) by forcing you to analyse your activities and future plans to ensure that time is spent on the fifth of essentials and not on the four-fifths of relatively trivial matters.

The plan must also recognize that accident plays a crucial part in the development of careers. According to one account, Theodore Geisel, famous among children all over the world as Dr Seuss, would never have written a children's book but for the chance that made him choose Flit, instead of a rival fly-spray, for use in a cartoon that appeared in the old comic magazine *Judge*. A top advertising man's wife saw the drawing and suggested Geisel to her husband as the ideal illustrator to work on the Flit account. Geisel's subsequent contract was so tightly drawn that children's books were the only activity which he could take up in order to fill his vacant hours.

We don't know, and neither does Geisel, whether Dr Seuss would ever have seen the light of day had it not been for the choice of Flit. All human events are chance, but the possession of talent and the determination to exploit that talent are by no means random. Pasteur's observation that 'fortune favours the prepared mind' is self-evidently true. Geisel was trying to make his name as a cartoonist in the first instance; he was good enough to land and hold a fat advertising contract in the second place (even though he never had a drawing lesson); and he was ambitious enough not to accept a soft life with Flit, a contract which only needed three months' work in a year.

When this combination of circumstances culminated in the writing of *And to think that I saw it on Mulberry Street*, moreover, Geisel produced a brilliant and original work. His subsequent 'learning-to-read' books were and are equally brilliant. His success came about not because he was lucky, but because he was very good – and good, moreover, in a well-chosen line of work. Being a marvellous editor of general interest picture magazines in our day, for instance, is a waste of time and ambition: nobody wants the product enough in preference to television.

Judgement of your own abilities has to be accompanied by sound judgement of the target at which you are aiming. The world's failures may be lacking on both counts, combining an inflated idea of their own talents with the pursuit an object which, even if they had the ability to reach it, simply wouldn't provide enough reward. If a person's self-judgement is warped to that extent, it's not easy to correct the defect or prevent the failure; even the simple tests of aptitudes and objectives won't work in these cases, because the failure doesn't want to learn any results that will contradict his own false image.

The tests, as always, come in the form of questions. On abilities: What have I done well (to my own satisfaction and that of others) in the past? What abilities do I think that I possess which have not been fully used in the past – and what evidence do I have that these talents are real? What defects have held me back? Can I take any action that will correct or remove those defects? What opportunities have I missed, and why did I miss them? What have I done badly in the past – and why? Am I, in any event, an ambitious person? (See page 130.)

The answers to such questions won't be as scientific, or perhaps as stimulating, as a psychologist's aptitude test; but they will provide a subjective profile that can be matched against ambitions. In most cases the value or worthlessness of the latter will be immediately obvious. Nobody has to wonder for long whether a vice presidency of General Motors is *worth* having: of course, it is. But the question of whether this or any other worthy objective is what you really want still has to be asked. For example, John DeLorean, a whiz-kid who was picked for the crucial job of running Chevrolet for the car giant, decided after a while that the big company life didn't suit him after all, and opted out.

He did not, however, retire to the lakes of Michigan to fish. DeLorean later re-emerged as a small-scale, would-be car tycoon in his own right. It wasn't business that drove him away from General Motors, but big business in the big corporation. To put it in over-simple terms, people like this become uncomfortable in their environment: and the wisest words of advice I ever received were 'Remember, any fool can be uncomfortable.' Sometimes, perhaps always, a trade-off is essential: so much discomfort in exchange for the experience or the money that can be traded in later, perhaps for greater comfort in this psychic sense.

The Courtship of Failure

It's as important to recognize what you dislike as it is to know what you want. A man isn't enviably successful who rises to the top in a profession he actually loathes – and it happens all the time. It follows that, if you hate all or part of your work, you should make doubly or trebly sure that you derive the maximum of whatever positive benefits are keeping you there. It could be that the benefits are negative: that you

The Ambition Quotient

ARE YOU, IN YOUR OPINION

an older person ....   a younger person........................

Did you have?

no university education................   some university education ....

Are you?

affected by feeling ....   emotionally stable, calm..............

shy, restrained ....   adventurous, socially bold ....

apprehensive, worrying.............   confident, self-assured ....

Do you have?

a low need for achievement........   a high need for achievement..........

Do you?

see change as negative................   see change as positive ....

Do you prefer?

shorter hours   more hours

with less travel ....   with more travel.........................

Are you?

satisfied with your   dissatisfied with super-

supervision and pay ....   vision and pay.............................

Do you get?

much work satisfaction   No..   Yes...

Are you?

locked in, stagnating   Yes.....   No..

Do you?

play it safe ....   enjoy a calculated risk ....

Do you spend?

much time with

superiors   No......................   Yes...

Is your career?

more successful than you   less successful than

hoped......................................   hoped..

Are you?

willing to move   more willing to move

Not very ....   Yes...

reasonably satisfied   Yes ......   No..

ill and away from work

quite often ....   not often....................................

affected by the stress

and tension of your job

Yes..   No..

Do you?

smoke quite a lot of

cigarettes, and take little

exercise   Yes ....   No..

Are you?

Type B ....   Type A .... (see p. 176)

The more ticks you scored on the left, the less ambitious you are: if all the ticks are on the right, your ambition is extremely high.

This chart is based on information from John H.Howard's article in *Management Today,* March 1978.

are frightened of the great wide world beyond the big company, that you simply lack the courage to tell the boss that you are quitting, above all that you fear failure. But success does not consist of the avoidance of failure. It's the other way round: the courtship of failure is the only route to exceptional success.

This may sound like a crazy paradox. But it encapsulates the true meaning of risk and the nature of professionalism. Any new project, from a business or a product to a new job, may fail. If it does, there are only two possibilities. Either the protagonist performed badly in the new task, or he made a mistake in starting the venture in the first place. This applies even if the decisive circumstances were beyond his control – like an obstructive board of directors, an unforeseeable collapse in the market, a sudden drying up of capital. OK: the flop wasn't his fault – except that, if he'd known all the facts beforehand, he wouldn't have gone ahead. So whose fault is it?

The true pro *always* takes the blame for everything that goes wrong within his orbit and tries to see where he, and not just the person primarily responsible, made his mistake – in order to avoid doing so again. He also works out a set of principles, proved in practice and flexible in application, that can be used time and again. No circumstances repeat themselves exactly, except one: the appearance in all chapters of your life story of one principal character, yourself. The more developed your sense and knowledge of how you best play that role, the better you will do – partly because repetition, as always, will tend to improve performance: up to the point when the act is obsolescent. But you will recognize that obsolescence if you have preserved the priceless gift of acknowledging error and listening to criticism. Nobody will ever criticise you, no matter how unfairly or even insanely, without the criticism containing at least a germ, if not a whole loaf, of valuable truth.

This resilience in the face of failure or possible failure is demonstrated in almost all the great success stories of our time – an epoch which has seen more success in more forms than all the rest of history put together. Edwin Land's Polaroid fortune developed from mistaken experiments to do with car headlights. The Tropicana orange juice king stumbled onto his gold-mine later in life, after several relatively abortive business ventures: the juice triumph sprang from just such an abortion in Florida, which left the entrepreneur stranded with nothing on his hands save time. The moral of such sagas isn't only that of Robert the Bruce and the spider – 'If at first you don't succeed, try, try again': nor even of its corollary – 'If at first you do succeed, keep on trying.' The lesson is rather that if you are going to fail because of inadequate or wrongly applied ability, it's vital to find out. Far better do that than go to the grave convinced that never in life did you ever exploit your talents to anything like the full.

That still leaves the vital question of how much risk you are prepared to run. For this, the tried and trusty fail-safe routine is the perfect answer. (See Chapter 6.) But this technique presupposes that you have worked out what the worst possible result can be – and for that matter, what is the best possible outcome, and what is the likeliest. You can put probabilities on these outcomes and make an even more refined judgement. Obviously, it makes no sense to change your job if the likeliest result is that you'll be no better off, and you know there's only a 100-1 chance that you'll get the chief executive spot: even if there is a comfortable fallback.

Pencil, Paper and Planning

The three Ps – pencil, paper and planning – will thus help to increase the chances of success and lessen those of failure. But the brain/mind will be doing its calculations and assessments of possibilities all the time, without conscious direction from its owner. The result is called a 'gut-feel' or a hunch. In the wonderful movie *Double Indemnity*, Edward G. Robinson played an insurance claims investigator who was alerted to skulduggery by the griping activity of a 'little man' in his stomach. For stomach, read skull, and you have the truth. Although hunches can be wrong, they are the end-result of marvellous mental processes, in which the super-computer, unbidden, has been running some of its most complex programmes. As noted in Chapter 6, never ignore a hunch. At the very least examine it as thoroughly as you would the advice of the best expert money can buy - if he happened to be advising against some course of action dear to your heart.

The advice of others may play a part in any success you win. Certainly, you're most unlikely to succeed without the help of other people: without, to be blunt, using them. The best form of using others is that which meets their life needs as successfully as it does your own. But you can't guarantee that; all you do know is that any individual's success is bound to benefit at least some of his associates, and that his failure is bound to damage some other people. So it's wrong for the successful man or woman to be stigmatized as a ruthless animal who climbs to fame and fortune on the backs of other people. If you think about it, there isn't much alternative – though there are plenty of ways of climbing without breaking other people's backs.

But you can't expect to be both highly successful and loved by all. The distrust of the careerist is in some part an expression of envy – and envy, as noted, can be destructive as well as a driving force, a canker or a fuel-injection system. The truly successful man – the Superman, if you will – directs his ambition inwards more than outwards. Like a well-balanced virtuoso musician, his concern is primarily with his own skills and his own last performance, not with whether Mtislav Rostropovitch or some other maestro makes a higher income. The most triumphant and brilliant pianist of his day, Franz Liszt, courted by impresarios as insatiably as he was by women, heard Paganini play the violin. Liszt was so overcome by what he saw as greater virtuosity that he fell to practising fourteen hours a day in an effort to raise his own fabulous technique to the standard of Paganini's. Envy had nothing to do with it; perfectionism, everything. The competitive urge at its finest and most useful is the urge to improve. Any improvement is a success. It follows that success lies not necessarily in being best (though that's a good thing to be) but in getting better – and in doing the best you can. Who can ask for anything more?

11.
Inside the Whale

FEW people can hope to use their personal and inter-personal skills only in personal relationships. For most of the time, especially in working time, impersonal relationships have the dominant influence on our lives. Persons, of course, are always involved, but we meet them only as representatives or parts of the impersonal organization in which we work, or study, or are members. The organization may not be greater than its parts, but it's bigger than we are – and it has a life and a personality (or impersonality) all its own.

The individual can choose to immerse himself completely in this larger-than-life, not entirely human creation. Group loyalty is an extremely powerful force in individual psychology. But total dedication to the company, the party, the union, or whatever, is becoming more unfashionable by the minute. It doesn't fit the prevailing social or spiritual ethos. There's even an elegant sociological theory which explains and identifies this phenomenon : the now famous distinction between Theory X and Theory Y management, as expounded by Douglas MacGregor and popularized by, among many others, Robert Townsend of *Up the Organization* and Avis ('we try harder') fame.

The Townsend version of how Avis was managed (while apparently lacking in historical accuracy) is the epitome of how the modern corporation would like to think it is managed. While Theory X is the old hierarchical military-style management – 'You do this or else' – the Theory Y school practises informality, consultation, the breaking down of barriers between people at different levels, the abolition of status symbols, the creation of genuine social equality and team work. But note that the Townsend version didn't propose any new ends or objectives for the new-style company. It was still dedicated to beating the pants off the competition, and to making as much money as possible for the top management and for the proprietors.

Setting that aside for the moment, note also that Theories X and Y bear an amazingly close similarity to two categories of the three involved in the theory of Transactional Analysis which, as Chapter 9 noted, holds that human attitudes can be classified as dominated by the Child, the Parent or the Adult. The authority-wielding, rule-forming Parent is obviously Theory X. The understanding, reasoning, supportive, sympathetic and liberal Theory Y plainly equates with the Adult. While Theory X maintains that the Child won't do as he should unless forced, Theory Y thinks the Child can be persuaded and led into adult behaviour.

All the same, it's still the organization and not the individual that determines the goals of the organization and sets the boundaries of individual freedom of movement and also achievement: witness the case of Avis. But nobody in his or her right (or normal) mind would prefer to live and work in a true-blue Theory X organization. Like the Nixon-Haldeman White House, any such outfit, in addition to being unpleasant to work for, rapidly breeds its own extremism. Since it is also out of keeping with the temper of the times, an X-style sweat-shop is likely to be in a state of permanent psychological crisis, and to have some trouble in finding sufficient X-inhabitants.

The Y-Style's Sure to Win

So the Y-style, in various gradations, is likely to prevail almost anywhere these days. Organizations are very quick to pick up social trends, especially if these are reflected in economic pressures. Thus, the public schools of England, once the most X-determined educational establishments on earth, all liberalized themselves at breakneck speed when failure to do so would rapidly have dried up the supply of fee-paying customers. That's the market at work. And one important question to ask about any organization offering employment is whether it is able and willing to respond to the voice of the market: in other words, to the demands of its environment.

That's because its responsiveness, or lack of it, will in turn greatly affect the fortunes and fate of those who work inside. Again, this doesn't apply only to large organizations (although most people will now belong in some fashion or other to organizations far greater in size than their grandparents could ever have imagined). At any level where people are grouped formally together, the members cannot follow their own self-interest, very obviously, unless it coincides with the collective interest. The advantage of smallness in this context is that it's easier to establish and identify with the collective interest in a small firm than it is with General Motors.

That's the root of another variant of the new management fashion in sociology, the breaking down of the big into small, discrete units, which are both more manageable and more human in scale. The

135

optimum size has tended to dwindle steadily in the post-war years: where 1,000 used to be thought the largest number you could have on one site, while preserving personal contact, the desirable figure, having paused at 500, is now generally put at 200. And even that 200 should, in theory, be fragmented in turn, until it's broken down into what the management writer Anthony Jay, in *Corporation Man,* has called 10-groups. (He identifies these with the primitive hunting party - not that it matters.)

This, then, is the revolving organizational stage on which the Self will have to deploy its talents. Again, note that it's nearly all given a context to which the individual must adapt, but which he cannot form or greatly influence save in exceptional circumstances. It's likely that life in organizations will continue to become more liberal and more decentralized and that it will probably give the individual more scope. But it will also place the individual under constraints – because that is the difference between organized and unorganized activity. So the crucial question for self-managers must stay the same: How can I exploit the organization to achieve my own personal objectives?

This isn't as anti-social as it might sound. Another theory of management, not so fashionable as it was, but still an abiding influence, holds that the key to organizational success is to identify the corporate and the individual objectives and tie them together. But this Management by Objectives is again a system imposed from outside (and above) the individual. The latter must still decide how to use the organization for his own ends, which doesn't imply any disloyalty. In fact, the chosen organization must not only be sensitive to the market (so that it doesn't leave you and the other members stranded on a sinking ship), but its general ethos must approximate to your own.

By insisting on market-sensitivity, I'm also establishing that one major part of the organizational ethos will be acceptance of change. Many people love settled order and like to think that the same desk in the same building will be theirs until retirement. It's possible, by making the right choice of job, to occupy this settled position within an organization that is itself changing all the time. But the outfit that attempts to provide universal stability of this kind will not only be dull, but doomed. Any change, even a shift of offices, is better than none: what's true of the individual personality is valid even for International Business Machines.

The choice of organization is strictly personal. If you're in the wrong place, doing the wrong thing, there's nobody else to blame. To find out if your organization fits you, and you fit the organization, see page 140. Suppose, like most people, you've made a reasonable choice. What's a reasonable course of action inside the organization? How should a member manage and develop himself to make the most of the mammoth (or the minnow, for that matter)? There's a one-word guide through the labyrinth: effectiveness.

Much of this book is concerned with increasing personal effectiveness. But to be effective within the organization has a different meaning from, say, improving cardio-vascular capacity or memory. These are internal achievements, while anything effective in an organization must be achieved outside the Self, and very probably outside the organization, too. But whether what's achieved is a better pension scheme for employees or a larger market share for the company's prime product, it must (if the individual is to know that he's been effective) be identifiable both in itself and as the individual's own work.

I'm lucky in this respect. I make magazines. Every publication day I see the product that we have all put together. We know the commercial results exactly, we can see what we've done well – and what we've done wrong. But we know what we're doing: and that phrase (in both senses) is the essence of effectiveness. You must have clear objectives; you must possess the means which are needed to reach those objectives; and you must have a method of establishing that those objectives have been met. Otherwise there's no chance of being effective, or knowing that you are.

The practice of effectiveness has been brilliantly described by Peter Drucker, whose personal influence on the evolution of the modern organization has been very great. What this approach means in corporate life can best be appreciated from one passage in Drucker's *The Effective Executive*. He's describing how you should select somebody for a job. The previous chapter discussed the horrors of firing; hiring, of course, is much more important, and partly for that very reason – if you need to fire somebody, it's nearly always the fault of whoever hired or promoted him in the first place. When you start life in organizations, being hired is a vital part of your career; but as you rise, hiring becomes progressively more important.

Four Questions for Hiring

Drucker says that there are four fundamental questions to ask about the candidate:

A What has he (or she) done well?
B What, therefore, is he likely to be able to do well?
C What does he have to learn or acquire to be able to get the full benefit from his strength?
D If I had a son or daughter, would I be willing to have him or her work under this person?
   (a) If yes, why?
   (b) If no, why?

137

Following a list of logical questions like this is itself an invaluable guide to effectiveness. The check-list may seem like a mechanical device. But time and again, running through a list of set questions about any aspect of a business or an organization will throw up areas of weakness, or at best confirm that you are on the right lines. The other important point about Drucker's catechism is that he has boiled the selection process down to essentials, placing his stress on what will ultimately count – the strengths of the individual. As Drucker says, you don't hire a man for his weaknesses (what he can't do) but for his abilities (where he is effective).

It follows that the most effective hirer and organization man is the one with the best subordinates. It's quite possible to hire somebody who is better than yourself. The most brilliant picker of men I ever knew made this his speciality; the result was to make him a superb success in his own job. Not only is it weak to shy away from the ambitious and able subordinate: it's terribly ineffective. Even in terms of self-preservation, a policy of rejecting talent is liable to be self-defeating, as your own deficiencies and those of your inferior associates get found out. This argument is even stronger in terms of rejecting advice; never refuse an idea, no matter where it comes from, if it happens to be the best one going – even if it kills an idea of your own.

This injunction is a tough one to follow, because we mostly invest too much of our own personality in our jobs and their content. If this is a problem, it can be mitigated by using what Townsend called the 'man from Mars' technique. You ask what a complete stranger would decide if the question were put before him. In other words, you try to exclude emotion. The fact that it's your pet scheme, say, isn't admissible: if it's not the best solution, too bad. If the emotion is not your own, but that of somebody else (especially your boss), then the problem is much tougher. It must still be faced.

The reasonable case must be pressed with every reasonable weapon at your disposal (including the Machiavellian methods suggested in Chapter 9). But if you're in no position to win, you'll be obliged at some point to accept defeat. If the matter is so stupendous that you are sure you cannot live with the results, then you go: that, too, is axiomatic. But organizational life can't be survived in comfort unless the member concerned concentrates his energy on what can be done and devotes as little energy as he can to the impossible. Lost causes can be every bit as time-consuming as victories: but they carry with them no satisfaction whatsoever, even if you were right.

This technique, of concentrating resources where they will be most effective, is indispensable. The management of time (Chapter 7) is basic. But it isn't just a question of staying away from committees wherever possible: it's also necessary to ensure, if you can, that any collective working group to which you belong concentrates its own resources. For a start, this means (a) providing all necessary information (i.e. what *they* want) to all those who are going to be vitally involved; (b) only taking up the time of those individuals on the subjects with which they are directly concerned; (c) where somebody has the authority of expertise, letting him use that skill and make the running in that area of the decision.

Decisions, decisions: problems, problems.

Not that organizations are exclusively dominated by taking decisions or solving problems (the two most common phrases used today). In the first place, the matters that are *not* decided may be more important than those which are: what's just left to carry on. Effectiveness requires systematic, periodic reviews of everything within your personal orbit, asking whether what's being done needs to be done at all; whether it's being done effectively; and whether it could be done more economically (of which more later). Organizations are continuous: they don't proceed from decision to decision in a series of kangaroo hops.

In the second place, talk of 'problems' in itself indicates a corporate anxiety neurosis. What's usually under consideration is not a problem, but a question: problems arise when questions are given the wrong answers, or where no feasible answer exists. If you can't meet the payroll on Friday, because you've run out of cash, and can't find any, that's a problem. But if you're considering what kind of management accounting system to install (which should stop you from running into that kind of cash flow problem), that is a *question,* to which several answers are possible. Choosing one is not a problem, but a necessity.

But still, decisions have to be made from time to time. A basic rule, as noted in Chapter 6, is never to take a decision that isn't necessary at all, or which doesn't have to be taken immediately, but to decide quickly when it is clear that a decision is inevitable. Delay only increases the chances of being right if the time is used for getting more information. Mostly, the delay merely reflects indecision or, worse still, indecisiveness. This usually results from fear: the procrastinator is worried in case the decision is wrong. Half of the time, it probably will be. But again, delay won't help. The decision-taker is far better advised to rely on fail-safe techniques. The basic question deserves repeating. If this goes as badly wrong as it possibly can, will the results be tolerable, for me and the organization? If the answer is No, then it's folly to proceed. Most great disasters in business have sprung from disregard of this question, coupled with failure to question the continuing efficiency of the operation. The question won't stop all disasters, however: if the organization is big and sound enough, it can survive a Ford Edsel or a Du Pont Corfam. Hindsight shows that both these failures could have been avoided by

139

The Organization and You

The organization to which you belong is in bad shape if any of the following questions get a consistent YES answer.

1   Is it impossible for people to plan their day, because they are always being called away for urgent matters?
2   Is the whole organization liable to alternations of elation/uproar in response to the same short-term stimulus (e.g. weekly sales figures)?
3   Are people continually made to drop what they are doing and report at once to superiors – or else?
4   Do the same emergencies recur again and again because the underlying causes are never removed?
5   Do important positions go unfilled for months?
6   Do people think of themselves as being in a rat race?
7   Do people, instead of saying what they think, disguise or conceal their opinions?
8   Is it difficult to reach you/your boss/your colleagues?
9   Do meetings conclude with a decision that it is premature to do anything at this time – that the best course is to 'Keep options open'?
10   Do people often have to postpone their holidays because they cannot be spared?
11   Are your actual hours of work, instead of being controlled by you, dictated by others – at your personal inconvenience?
12   Do you/other people have to remake travel and other arrangements a great deal?
13   Are people generally more concerned with how good they look, not how good they are?
14   Do those in charge think only rarely of (a) the future (b) personnel policies (c) rewarding good work?
15   Are people denied information which affects them directly?

Any YES is a symptom of organizational disorder, which you should seek to rectify if possible. If the total YES count reaches 5, the organization is probably beyond help. If the count is 10, there have to be very strong reasons for your staying there at all.

You and the Organization

You are coping well with life inside the whale if you can answer YES to the following eight questions.

1   Do you delegate authority and not insist on making every decision?
2   Can you make a firm decision after a reasonable amount of deliberation?
3   Can you take stock of yourself and objectively view your own assets and liabilities?
4   Are you able to listen and learn from others? (The opposite is to jump the gun in conversations and think only of what you have to say next.)
5   Are you able largely to ignore the occasional barbs of sharpshooters and unkind critics who would undercut you?
6   Do you stay reasonably calm and controlled in dealing with subordinates? (The opposite is habitually to lose your temper when irritated.)
7   Do you relate on a purely personal level and have at least two or three good friends in your occupation?
8   Are you able to forget the job in favour of your family once the day's work is done?

If you answer no to three or more of these questions – and admit that the no answer applies over a reasonable period of time – then you need some self-searching and maybe some outside help. You may have a budding emotional problem, or one that you've covered up for years.

These charts (above and opposite) are based on articles in *Fortune* magazine and *Business Week*.

proper application of the analysis techniques which were recommended in Chapter 6. But Corfam, at least, fitted Peter Drucker's rules for identifying priorities in taking executive decisions.

These are '(1) pick the future as against the past; (2) focus on opportunity rather than on problems; (3) choose your own direction – rather than climb on the bandwagon; and (4) aim high, aim for something that will make a difference rather than for something that is "safe" and easy to do.' The fact that, Du Pont's synthetic leather, if not Ford's middle-priced car, met these four criteria, and still failed lamentably, makes another important point. You can't win 'em all. Some degree of failure is inevitable, and no career, inside or outside an organization, can be built on avoiding failure. You have to aim for success.

The inevitable failures can actually help to achieve success, so long as you're prepared to learn the lessons that failure always has to teach. It would be amazing, for instance, if Ford ever launched a new car after the Edsel without the benefit of up-to-the-minute market research. It's much easier to confront your own past mistakes than to face your present fears. Experience is an excellent teacher, whether the experience is good or bad, and the over-riding essential of self-development within the organization is to obtain and learn from experience. It's that which builds up a set of techniques and approaches for the organization member to carry around wherever he goes.

The kit will need adaptation to suit different conditions. But you need to evolve both the equipment and the style which suit you, your job and your organization – and which work. As noted at the start of this chapter, the kit these days is most unlikely to contain a high proportion of Theory X material – though it must have *some*. You can't expect to be a nice guy all the time; hard, even authoritarian measures and stances sometimes have to be taken. But in general you will probably have to be a Y-man, like it or not. The odds are that you will like it, because that is what you are conditioned to like and because it's mostly common sense.

Consider these observations:

> 1 Trouble with employees (like bad time-keep-ing and poor quality work) may be the company's fault rather than that of the men and women concerned.

> 2 You get better results from managers if you set them targets, get them to agree those targets, and reward them for success.

3 A bad environment (dirty canteen, bad ventilation, etc) will tend to produce bad work. But a good environment is only the precondition for getting good performance – that depends on the work itself.

4 Building up the capacities of the people in the company, and getting better results from them, is as valuable as improving the plant and machinery or the product portfolio.

5 Once people feel adequately paid and reasonably secure, they start to get more interested in what they are doing and in how much satisfaction they can get out of doing it.

6 You can run your company either on the assumption that people have to be forced to work properly, or on the belief that, properly encouraged, they will perform well without the need for coercion.

Simplified in this way, the thoughts don't seem very revolutionary. The gurus, from top to bottom, are Chris Argyris, Peter Drucker, Frederick Herzberg, Rensis Likert, Abraham Maslow and the aforementioned Douglas McGregor. They all have the same general drift: treat people positively and humanely and you should get positive results. Or do unto others as you would be done by - to quote again a far more ancient source of behavioural wisdom.

The easy-going, anyway, have an easier life. But there's one area in which you must be as hard as any Theory X taskmaster: that of professional performance. If you accept less than the best professional standards you can achieve in the circumstances, and if you fail to develop your professional powers, neither you nor the organization, by definition, are getting as much as they should from your presence. Moreover, a high level of professional performance helps to solve the main inter-personal problem of organizational life: personal acceptance.

The Independent Eccentric

A high degree of eccentricity and independence will be tolerated if the independent eccentric is indisputably able in some role vital to the organization. It's the authority of expertise referred to before. Add to it the Y-type attributes of helpfulness and acceptance of others, and your own acceptance will seldom be in doubt. This isn't the same thing as seeking popularity, which has nothing to do with effectiveness, just as effectiveness needn't have much to do with efficiency. It doesn't do anybody any organizational good to run supremely well on the same spot: similarly, to be well liked in itself wins no prizes.

In most organizations, the prizes are both social and economic, usually combined. The man with the highest salary and perquisites is normally the man with the highest status, at which level he may well(like a bishop or a top politician) deplore the crass materialism of others. There's nothing intrinsically wrong, however, with seeking the highest reward, or the most the traffic will bear, for yourself or for the organization. On the contrary: what's intrinsically wrong is the opposite – to lose or to waste the organization's money. Economic operation, as mentioned before, is essential, because the organization is ultimately the sum of its resources. Spend more of those resources than are being renewed, and the organization must eventually die. Bring in more resources than are being expended, however, and it will live for ever.

The expression of this truth in money language (see Chapter 12) only complicates a simple issue. Even organizations which are wholly financed by the taxpayer have expenditure of resources on one side of the account, and benefits provided on the other. If the benefit value doesn't outweigh the cost, sooner or later that organisation will be doomed. There's a humdrum accountancy phrase which exactly sums up the situation: to 'make a contribution' means to provide a sum in excess of outgoings – an amount which can then be applied to the overheads of the organization. In the end, the laws of economics demand that all organizations make a contribution or cease to exist. Much the same rule applies to the organization member: for his own sake as well as the organization's, he must contribute.

Which is only another way of saying that he must be effective. There's always the temptation, of course, to believe that your own survival in office is vital to the well-being of the organization, so that you can justifiably devote all your energies to that end. It's a delusion. Remember that nobody is indispensable. While it will do you no harm for others to believe that, without you, nothing is possible, it will certainly harm you to have any such idea. Organizations go on and on. Individuals don't – and that's the essential philosophical starting point for the conduct of a life inside the whale.

144

12.
It's Not Only Money

THE similarity between human attitudes to money and sex has often been remarked. Both subjects are surrounded by taboos. It's no more decent to discuss your money or money problems in certain circumstances than to boast or complain about your sexual performance at a P.T.A. meeting. Just as many (perhaps most) people feel or fear that others have a richer, better sex-life than themselves, so nearly everybody believes that money is a mystery which others understand more fully – which is why they become richer than us. An aura of obscenity hangs over excesses of either lust or lucre. In fact, money is about the only fairly general inanimate object of lust.

The psychological explanations of this strange similarity offer a fascinating trail through the unconscious; but for the self-manager the most important starting point is to recognize how simple money really is. Unlike sex, a simple physical act infinitely complicated by its emotional networks, money is simple arithmetic unadorned by any complexities. It stands as a proxy for all manner of emotions, of course. But nobody need fear that he or she lacks basic competence. If you can master arithmetic at an elementary level, you can master money. Algebra, the differential calculus, and so forth are all totally unnecessary. Money is adding, subtracting, dividing and multiplying – and that truly is all.

As with most skills, from riding a bicycle to flying a plane, the ability to handle money depends first on abolishing or overcoming fear. Money itself is nothing: an opaque substance, useful only when transmuted into something else. It is an expression of other activities. For most people, most of their money comes from their earnings: from the exchange of their skills or labour for the means to obtain the skills or labour of others. On the whole, this aspect of money is by far the best understood. We usually have a reasonable idea of the market value of whatever we have to sell, and an even more accurate idea of how much of our selling price is needed to pay for the standard of living required. When a man is nervous about asking his boss for a raise, the reason is fear of the former, or fear of being rejected: not fear of money.

How to Manage Your Finances

Nobody's financial control, in a business or a family, can be efficient without a proper cash flow statement and balance sheet. These take priority over a budget, because they set the boundaries within which the budget must operate. Both are illustrated on pages 148-9. You should have last year's detailed figures as a base for next year's workings, because the key to control is to compare results with the original projections, or estimates. But it's also possible to start from scratch, as long as you don't fall into over-optimism on either income or outgo when it comes to making the estimates.

Once you've filled in the pair of tables, you will know how much cash is available for the year, over and above the items already included. You can then fill in the budget – which should always include a significant amount (say, 10 per cent) for contingencies. It isn't possible to say what are the ideal proportions for other budget allocations, since it depends on many variables, such as the absolute level of income. The higher the income, the greater the proportion set aside for saving is the general rule. But you shouldn't be spending more than 15 per cent on food; 5 per cent on clothing; 5 per cent on recreation; less than 5 per cent on life insurance; less than 5 per cent on savings; more than 25 per cent on all fixed housing costs.

The difficulties arise partly in spending, or over-spending. For most people, expenditure has an unpleasant habit of mounting to the level of the available income, if not somewhat higher. (It's a financial equivalent of Parkinson's Law, which holds that work always expands to fill the time available.) The remedy for this condition is to consider the family or the personal affairs as a business, and to proceed by annual budgets, based on a cash flow forecast and broken down by quarters or months, with amounts provided for contingencies. All expenditure is then faithfully recorded, all income duly entered. Finally, you keep a balance sheet showing the overall position at the end of each accounting period, which, of course, should coincide with each tax period (see pages 148-9).

None of these stages is especially hard or needs much time. But very few people do it – doubtless because of the sexual nature of inhibitions about money. After all, nobody would think of trying to run a business without orderly financial accounts (although you wouldn't think so from the appearance of some businesses). Personal finances have just as much need of order and efficiency. Nor is there any substitute, again, for pencil or pen and paper. You have to set it down and you have to get it right: otherwise you can't be sure that your finances are under control.

So far the principles are little different from those which Mr Micawber would have understood. But modern man has to cope with two financial sophistications, like it or not. One is debt: the other, tax. (If you're really out of luck, they may come to one and the same thing.) The most prudent of people are likely to be in debt: principally on their house, but maybe on a business as well. In fact, some of the world's wealthiest men make it a point of honour to be in debt at all times, and never to have cash in hand. That's the kind of remark that makes your typical income-earner turn up his toes in horror. But it's another arithmetical simplicity.

Suppose (a nice supposition) that you own a business worth a neat million. A safe, conservative Victorian would live off the proceeds in contentment. Today's millionaire knows that the business can borrow money internally, so to speak – that is, the banks will provide its working capital and investors (mostly big institutions) will subscribe investment capital. At the same time, our millionaire's personal shares are highly acceptable collateral for loans from banks which will fall over themselves to oblige. So he can afford to borrow half a million (knowing that his dividends will easily cover the interest costs) and invest or spend it, as he wishes. He doesn't have to budget his spending, because the bank loan can go up and down according to circumstances.

No Magic in Borrowing

Note that the system begins to crack and creak if the value of the investments (including the man's own shares) starts to drop, or his income fails to cover his interest costs. Being rich doesn't remove the necessity of being efficient, as spendthrift heirs like Huntington Hartford have discovered to their intense pain. But suppose that the millionaire borrows half a million for the business, too, buying a new machine for that amount and putting up profits by half in consequence. The interest

Cash flow statement

	Personal cash flow for (year)											
Income												
Salary												
Interest, dividend												
Wife's income												
Other												
Cash receipts total (A)												
Disbursements												
Taxes												
Pension contrib.												
Other												
Total												
Take home cash												
Interest payments												
Rates												
Living expenses												
Other												
Total (B)												
Net cash before debt amortisation and saving (A-B)												
Bank debt												
Mortgage principal												
HP debt												
Savings												
Insurance												
Total (C)												
Net spendable income												

Personal balance sheet

	Actual (opening date of period)		Estimated (closing date)	
Assets				
Current assets				
Cash &				
Building society				
Investments				
Securities				
Insurance				
Pension rights				
Other				
Total				
Fixed and other long-term assets				
House				
Personal property				
Other				
Total				
Liabilities				
Bank debt				
Mortgage				
Other				
Total				
Net worth				
Total liabilities and net worth				

costs (at 10 per cent, for arithmetical convenience) are £50,000. That provides extra pre-tax profits of £50,000 on the assumption that the business was earning £200,000 a year before the new machine came on stream. The shares are now worth £250,000 more, in theory, and neither the borrowing inside the business, nor that on his personal account, have reduced the man's fortunes by a cent: quite the reverse. There's no magic in the process, which is exactly how innumerable middle-class people have built up estates on property deals: that is, they have bought their own homes on borrowed money.

If a house is bought for £20,000 and sold ten years later for £40,000, the purchaser has made 100 per cent on his money. But if the house had been financed entirely on borrowed money, all the profit would still have gone to the purchaser – only, since none of his own capital had been involved, his return would have been astronomical: while his unspent £20,000 (assuming that he had it) could have been earning still more money somewhere else. The key is only that the net interest paid on the borrowing ('net' meaning after tax) must be lower than the return (in this case, the capital gain) on the investment. The house grew in value by 7 per cent annually: so long as the net interest cost was lower, the investor was bound to make a higher return by borrowing than by putting all his cash in the one basket.

As you can see, it's not a very difficult concept. But it enshrines a trap into which many good and true people fall. The device of borrowing to beef up the returns on your own capital is known as 'gearing' to the British and 'leverage' to the Americans. Either way, the words graphically explain what the borrower is up to. He increases the power of his own resources by, in one metaphor, moving into higher gear, so that one turn of his own monetary pedal produces more turns of the wheel: or, following the American line of thought, using a lever so that far less financial pressure at the investor's end will move a greater weight at the business end.

Very obviously, £20,000 growing at 7 per cent annually will double your money in ten years. (A delightful rule is that by dividing any interest rate into 70, you'll find the rough time it takes to generate a 100 per cent gain by the apparent magic of compound interest – of which more later.) If, however, you can borrow an extra £20,000 as well, the gain will be greater; but only if that golden rule is observed. *The simple interest paid must be less than the compound interest (or capital gain) received.*

Our happy investor with his £20,000 profit would be much less happy if his borrowed £20,000 cost him 14 per cent. Over ten years, he would have to fork out £28,000, and his profit would shrink to £12,000. There are circumstances in which this loss of profit would be tolerable: if, for instance, the total price-tag on the investment was £40,000, and it was a case of all or nothing. But there, too, a cautionary rule applies: if the total return on the investment is less than the interest due, the investor starts to eat up more than his original capital. In other words, there's no conceivable way in which a money-losing investment can be turned into a successful one by financial wizardry alone. Just as Micawber said, income must exceed outgo.

It doesn't matter, of course, what form the income takes. If other people thrust so-called equity capital into your project, it can survive (like many American gee-whiz companies of the Soaring Sixties) through year after year of absent profits. That's because you can use the equity money to pay the bills without incurring any obligation to repay the funds to the suckers. With banks and other providers of fixed interest capital, the case is different: they usually take steps to ensure that first come (themselves) are served when it comes to distributing any income or (if the concern is liquidated) sharing out any assets.

Watch that Gearing

The harsh effect of gearing and leverage is best shown in stock market and commodity speculation. Borrow £20,000 to match your own capital, and you're laughing if the investment doubles. If it halves, however, you've lost not just £10,000 of your original capital, but the whole lot. The bank will still want its £20,000, and whatever you've bought is now only worth that amount. Once again, the lesson is simple: safe borrowing rests on safe employment of capital. House loans are the perfect example, since the value of homes in prime locations rarely falls over the lifetime of the mortgage, and the value of the householder's price on the property should always be comfortably above the amount of the loan.

It follows that anybody whose debts (including things like the unpaid capital and interest on instalment loans) are not amply covered by the realizable worth of the family assets is in an uncomfortably exposed position. A key word here, by the way, is 'realizable'. Usually debts are very precisely spelt out in money terms: but the value of family heirlooms, even family homes, is customarily exaggerated by their proprietors. A useful rule of thumb in such matters is to halve whatever value you are fond of quoting to visitors. Paper values are worth nothing, even as paper; and nothing has any value until it is exchanged for that value.

So the mystery of debt evaporates. It is used by rich men because they can cover their borrowings easily with their collateral, and because they can earn more on the borrowed money than they need pay out in interest. Sometimes they can generate those higher earnings because they have access to forms of investment which aren't available to the poorer mortal. Only a Richard Burton can buy Elizabeth Taylor a diamond as big as the Ritz; lovely tax-free instruments like Eurobonds, or marvellous shares like those in the Hoffman La Roche drug firm, are denominated in sums so large that small investors aren't in the game: great farms, fast horses, Old Masters – many and various are the items that only the rich can buy.

But the relatively poor should waste little self-pity on this fact. What generally makes these items attractive is precisely what makes them expensive: that they are in very limited supply. If the supply were large enough to satisfy everybody who wanted a Rembrandt, the price of that wonderful man's works would immediately plummet. That's where the prodigiously productive Picasso showed his commercial wisdom: tightly controlling the amount of his work which actually came onto the market.

The leverage (to use that word again) which the wealthy derive from their wealth also applies in the matter of compound interest. This simply means that, if money is continuously reinvested, the interest paid earns interest in turn. Thus an investment yielding 10 per cent for seven years doesn't yield 70 per cent in total, but 100 per cent, or thereabouts. Apply this happy little formula to £100 and the money adds £100: let the figures rise to £100 million, and the possessor can earn fabulous rewards without effort, even though precisely the same arithmetic is at work. In fact, if compound interest is allowed to work unhindered on a large enough sum, it must eventually rise to unimaginable totals: that £100 million, for instance would be worth £13 billion within fifty years.

But the magic doesn't work, of course, unless you do in fact re-invest the income, while also leaving the capital intact. Moreover, the yield never rises above 10 per cent, even though it appears to do so. You are only receiving higher returns because you are investing more money each year. Points like these only mystify people because the very simple principles are described in numbers, arithmetical symbols rather than words; and the numbers, to those who are not especially numerate, have a numbing effect.

The solution is to think through the proposition in words. For instance, take the advertisements that sometimes appear in the British Press extolling the charms of investments for high tax-payers: and the latter don't come any higher than in Britain. If a man's tax rate is 98 per cent, £100 of income is equivalent to the yield on £5,000. So a tax-free sum of £100 on a £1,000 investment could be described as the same thing as a taxable yield of 500 per cent, which is what the ads duly said. But any investor who thought he would receive 500 per cent was in for a rude shock. All he got was £100: or 10 per cent.

Express it in words, and any mystery disappears. If the income had been the taxable result of an investment (*which it was not*), it would have required a vastly larger amount of capital to produce that income. The vital words are *which it was not*. That being so, you can obviously ignore the whole proposition, can't you? The principle is only valuable if the investor is comparing different forms of investment with varying rates of return and various degrees of tax liability. Then he obviously goes for the one offering the highest 'grossed-up' yield, that being the technical jargon – because that, by definition, will yield the largest amount of cash-in-hand.

It isn't quite as easy as that, since the fat cat will also have to consider the time factor: when the different investments he's considering will produce their respective payments. Ordinary people have been caught by the fact that money is time (and not the other way round) ever since financiers have been operating among the public at large. In many countries laws have now been brought in to curb the abuse which had people paying 10 per cent on loans when (because the amount of the loan outstanding was reducing over time) the real rate of interest was far higher.

It's also true that a rate of 2 per cent a month must be higher than 24 per cent a year, because the lender has use of your interest payments (which means that you don't) for longer periods. All of us are always making presents to institutions by allowing them to hold our money for periods of time ranging from days to years, without making the holders pay anything for the privilege. In fact, sometimes we pay *them*: we pay more than the face value for travellers' cheques – but the bank, or American Express, or whoever else issued them doesn't have to turn any money over until we cash the cheque: and that could be a month later, even on a normal holiday.

The Lines of Financial Defence

The well-managed self-financier keeps the amount of his money which earns no income at minimum levels. He'll need some working balance in a current account at the bank, but the budgeting recommended above will determine exactly what that reserve should be. Behind the first-line defences, he'll need a second line, to be mobilized speedily if extraordinary expenditure should be needed: that should be the safe investment that currently offers the highest yield. Behind that, the third line, come the medium- and long-term investments on which money can be borrowed if the chance of a lifetime (like a cut-price Monet) turns up, and cash is needed in large amounts: blue-chip bonds and insurance policies come into this category.

Beyond that are the growth investments: the commodities, art works, stocks, stakes in private companies – anything which might augment the family fortune (a home, perhaps the best investment of all, is taken for granted). What you actually invest in is a matter of choice. But it helps to forget one old rule and to remember a new one. The has-been rule is, the greater the risk, the higher the return. This is true of fixed interest investments – if somebody is offering twice the going rate, don't take it: somewhere or other, there's an unacceptable risk. But the return on equities and a whole pile of other growth investments over the past decade has been lower than on much safer categories. The essence of such investments is volatility: and to make money from volatile investments, you must *manage* them, almost on a day-to-day, certainly on a week-to-week basis.

Before discussing what this implies, here's the new rule – the best growth investment is the garden you till yourself. Most of the world's greatest investments have been made by men in their own businesses. You may get lucky and find a friend who will do as well for you (or better) than you could yourself. But don't bank on it. Equally, if you are investing in collectable items, from wine to early inn-signs, buy things you really care for and know about. Otherwise, not only are you likely to lay an egg – you will deserve to.

In every case, moreover, remember that you don't usually have to deal. Far fewer people have been ruined by failing to make a deal than have been crucified by a bad bargain. If you do deal, try to find an objective basis for the price you pay. An English hotelier, paying a for-tune for a brewery, rationalized the price by calculating how much he was paying for each of the hundreds of fine old English pubs in the deal. It worked out at a mere £50,000 per pub – a figure which, he was sure, had to be cheap. It's the fail-safe principle again: what you pay will be determined by what the seller thinks the market will bear. He won't sell for less than he thinks he can get; and if you offer more than he believes it to be worth, that by definition determines what the traffic will bear. Your safeguard in these circumstances is to seek confirmation of your price – like the hotelier just mentioned.

In buying choice objects of your fancy, the fail-safe fallback is the delight you get from possession. How much you pay, provided you can afford it, is subordinate to this joy. But that noble attachment has no place in financial investments. *Never* get emotionally involved with a company in which you own stock – unless it really is your business. The great virtue of stocks is that they go up and down. Thus anybody who buys at the bottom and sells at the top, and goes on doing so, will make a fortune regardless of what happens to the Dow Jones, the F.T. index or any other of the crunched numbers that measure the performance and vitality (or debility) of the stock markets of the world. As 1977 drew to its close, shares in Shell, one of the world's greatest industrial companies, stood at a price 15 per cent below their high and 18 per cent above their low – there's enormous room for profitable action in such hard facts. But unless you didn't care whether you bought or sold Shell, only caring for the profit you sought, that profit could never have been won.

The principles for exploiting investment opportunities of this nature use many key items of the Superman kit. First, fix an objective. How much money do you want to make? In sum and as a percentage gain? Second, fix a fail-safe fallback. How much are you prepared to lose? Third, if you're betting on a higher price for a stock or the market, ask (and answer honestly) what reason you have for supposing that the price will indeed go up.

Going Against the Crowd

There's another of those useful golden rules here: by and large, stock markets follow the trend of interest rates – or rather, move against that trend. If rates go up, markets go down; and it works just as effectively the other way round. You need a very convincing argument to go against this rule – and the one argument you should never accept is the action of the mass. It stands to reason that more money will always be made by the man who goes against the crowd. It's all a matter of timing.

The timing is easier if you know what you are trying or hoping to achieve from investment. If it was £1,000, or 25 per cent appreciation within four weeks, reaching the target gives an automatic sell signal. You are, of course, free to revise your target at any time; but never waste any self-pity on the gain that got away. There will always be great escapes – nobody could possibly take advantage of every opportunity. You should only reproach yourself if either you've been doing absolutely nothing (out of idleness or preoccupation with other matters), or if you have been investing without a plan and without keeping the meticulous, honest account of your investments that you need for that plan.

That simply means recording accurately every penny you paid for an investment – including brokerage and any other expenses. This cuts the other way when accounting for sales. There's no other rational foundation – and there's no route to an investment pay-off that doesn't involve work, brainwork with those tried and trusted friends, pencil and paper. Of course, unless you're a professional, the time you spend in this way will be limited. But it should be a fixed time every week – not every month, since events often move too fast for you. It could be, unfortunately, that your targets are always missed on what the pros call the upside, that you all too often find yourself selling to take your previously determined maximum loss.

If so, recognize the fact that, just as some are born beautiful and others aren't, some simply have no gambling luck, or anything like it. For such as these, there's only one law – don't gamble, and don't whatever you do, succumb to the belief that there is an investment waiting round the corner that combines total safety with the highest possible return. There isn't, and those who tell you otherwise are almost certainly crooks, con-men on the make. If you can't gamble, steer clear of stocks, commodities and casinos: but you can still reap some handsome monetary rewards – as can gamblers – with no risk at all.

Suppose that you have £20,000 net worth, and reap the £1,000 target harvest mentioned. The net result after British capital gains tax will be £700 extra in the kitty - and that, if you think about it, has been the be-all and end all of the exercise – a gain of 3.5 per cent in your net worth compared with what it might otherwise have been. That is the final outcome of all investment programmes, indeed, of all earning and spending. The same result can be achieved in ways other than capital gains. You can spend less or earn more. You can pay less tax. If your family holiday would have cost £800, but you borrow a friend's villa or cottage and only spend £100, your potential net worth has been improved by just as much as your flutter in the stock market.

The essential discipline is to include in the annual budgeting a target for increase in net worth. How you hit that bulls-eye is then a matter of choice – though the obvious point is that no easier method of wasting money exists than paying more tax than you have to. You may be lucky (especially if you are rich) and find an adviser who will save you from this fate. But almost certainly there is no substitute for homework – for finding out yourself what ways of minimising tax are available to you (legally, of course) and for making sure that you use those methods. Here, too, it's useful to have a target: the amount of tax, as a proportion of gross income, that *you* (and not the State) feel it's proper, right and decent to pay.

The word 'homework' in the last paragraph probably holds part of the clue to the money mystery. From early days in school, for most children, arithmetic is bound up with unpleasant tasks, sums done wrong, unhappy comparisons with the greater skill of others. Couple this with the efforts of parents to instil respect for money into the young, throw in the normal human reluctance to face hard facts (like that you can't afford a new car), and you can begin to understand why otherwise rational people make a mess of their own material business.

In terms of gratification for time expended, doing your personal accounts ranks very low; but in terms of practical benefit, it can rank far higher than household repairs. The sexual analogy holds good. Once inhibition has been overcome, and repetition has been established, the intimidating becomes the familiar, the frightening becomes the comforting. Yet money, of all the forces that affect human life, is the easiest to control, because the emotion invested in it is purely artificial. Money is neutral, a means to an end, to be employed as a tool. It will work better, like any tool, if it's kept bright, shining and sharp by regular maintenance. If you don't know what you are worth, or exactly what you earned last year, or what you spend, or what your investments have yielded down the years – then you are not looking after your money weapon and deserve to see it rust in spots.

Of course, it can be attacked by outside enemies – in particular inflation. If your accounting is to be strictly honest, it should re-cast all the figures in constant money: say, 1970 currency. That way, when your income doubles, you tell yourself that 'in real terms' it has stayed exactly the same. But the exercise has no purpose other than to depress you. You have to pay your bills in current money, which is what you will be paid in. You can't hope to outrun anything more than a modest inflation by investing. You simply have to accept that, in inflationary times, your targets for increase in net worth and income have to be adjusted higher and higher.

The 'real money' concept, however, is one of those clever ideas which fog the mind. For one thing, there's no such thing as an accurate measure of inflation. For another, prices are constantly changing in relation to each other. In most countries, the price of labour has risen faster than that of goods in almost every post-war year – and much faster than some goods. That's why standards of living have risen: to talk about prices rising in this context must be misleading. What inflation does destroy is the value of savings; but even this concept isn't as simple as it sounds. If you own a millionth of I.B.M., you don't own any less of it because the money in which that particle is denominated has lost buying power in terms of a basket of groceries. In 'real' terms, your millionth obviously becomes 'worth' more year by year. What should concern you is only whether the current money invested in your share of I.B.M. couldn't be better applied at current values elsewhere. As with every other mystery of money, inflation only requires thought to lose its intellectual terrors. And thinking is the super-machine's cheapest resource.

13. The Strain of the Day – and Night

CALL an activity stressful, or say to a man that he is under stress, and you've obviously condemned the first and criticized or warned the latter. Observe a great conductor driving an orchestra through Beethoven's Fifth, however, or an ace racing driver powering his way round a Grand Prix circuit, and admiration is unbounded. Yet both are quite plainly under stress – the adrenalin is pumping through the blood-streams at a tearing pace, the heart-beats are correspondingly elevated, the sweat is probably pouring off the foreheads: why don't we urge them to ease off – after all, any businessman showing the same physiological pattern would be thought to be in imminent danger of a coronary thrombosis?

The answer is that stress gets confused with strain. Any endeavour that stretches human capacity is bound to be both stressful and (obviously) exceptionally rewarding in terms of human output. Seen from this angle, stress is positively beneficial: no stress, no achievement. Sex is a perfect example. Measured by its effects on the adrenal flow, the heart-beat and various other functions, intercourse is as stressful an activity as could be found. Yet people commonly suppose that sexual satisfaction is wonderfully therapeutic. In physiological terms, however, the symptoms of sexual stress are identical to the deplored signs of executive pressure.

As in the case of sex, the physical stress is inseparable from the achievement. No strain, no orgasm. Plainly, stress is not a simple matter, and the only simple observation that can be made on the subject is that, rather than stress itself, the ability to cope with the stress is the crucial factor. Moreover, it's an error, possibly a fatal one, to assume that a condition of high stress means that you are in high gear. It's very easy to get worked up over nothing, day after day.

To put it another way, emotions centred on the subject at hand are essential. Emotions which ostensibly arise from the subject, but have nothing fundamental to do with it, are often destructive – not only to the person concerned, but to his or her victims. The classic case is the bullying boss who terrorizes his subordinates. The method may be effective for a surprisingly long time in terms of getting results. But it eventually must reduce the staff either to people who crave bullying, or to those who have been subjected to it for so long that they are crippled by the battering.

Masochists and walking wounded do not make the most efficient subordinates. So the emotional self-indulgence of the tyrant must sooner or later hurt his chances of achieving his real objectives (assuming that maltreating others isn't what he really wants to do). The chances of avoiding excessive or ill-directed strain and stress are increased by reducing the areas about which you allow yourself to feel strained or stressed. The basic questions for all human activity apply. What am I trying to achieve? How can I achieve it? Am I achieving what I've set out to achieve? Any emotional expenditure outside the framework of the answers is wasted.

But the healthy stress which you may not even notice – like the concentration of mind and body that accompanies successful work – isn't the problem. The activity concerned solves the stress problem of itself. The vital point to remember, though, is that every human being has a limit to the amount of effort that mind and body (or both combined) can endure. The most you can achieve with the least effort is the ideal. Many of the devices described in this book – for efficient use of time or study, say – also help to reduce strain. So do organization and method in general – the very process of tidying up, sitting down, planning, arranging is therapeutic. But the best therapy of all, of course, is not to overdo stressful activity.

Most, if not all people, have early tangible warnings of over-stress: pains in the gut, agony in the back (tension causes far more back pain than 'rheumatism', slipped discs, badly designed chairs or anything else – see Chapter 14), spots and sores, scaling fingers, red blotches. When the tell-tale signs appear, stop. Sleep more, nap more, put off more, slow down the tempo – and put into practice some of the preventive and restorative methods which I'm about to recommend, and all of which work. The approach is the same whether the strain is the result of a prolonged period of overwork; or if the stress is one of those strange fits which, seeming to come from nowhere, leave the victim trembling and shaken; or if an emotional crisis is the cause. In all cases, the stress takes two forms – physical and mental.

How Exercise Helps

The former can be measured on various scales: the amounts of adrenalin or lactic acid in the bloodstream; the blood pressure; the pulse rate. The heart can raise its beat by a quarter purely in response to a few words – no wonder the ancients thought that it was the site of the emotions. Sweating in states of fear and anxiety is another familiar symptom. Since these are physical signs, however, they can obviously be treated at the physical level – and vigorous physical exercise, as noted in Chapter 3, both helps to limit stress and, quite literally, to work it off.

This probably explains the addictive affect of running or jogging programmes. The runner craves the relief which he obtains, not by ingesting powerful chemicals, but by using them up. Since exercise raises oxygen consumption, and that increases the rate of lactic acid metabolism, the connection is direct. The great attraction of running, too, is that the energetic and rhythmic movement tends to obliterate thought. Games in which there is a waiting element, even squash, do not suppress anxiety so completely, at least during play. On the other hand, hitting something hard (even if it's an object as small as a squash or golf ball), while taking on a 'shadow' opponent in a game (rather than a real enemy in life), is à harmless way of releasing aggressive tensions – and still building up the vital oxygen-consumption rate. Using the blood pressure test, one American experimenter put patients suffering from hypertension on six months of alternating running and jogging. He found an average drop in blood pressure of over 12 points – and that was with no other change in their habits or regimes. Since at the age of 45 every 10 point rise in blood pressure takes three years off life expectancy, the advantages of reducing stressful symptoms in this way are obvious.

At the opposite pole from exercise is relaxation, though the two are closely related. Watch a boxer slumping on his stool between rounds: all the muscles that have been tensed up for three minutes of violent action let go, flop; the head lolls around. This, as it happens, embodies the basic principle of relaxation. To relax a muscle, first make it tense. You then know when it relaxes, and what relaxation feels like. The most effective general relaxation procedure I know is the basic yoga exercise known as 'the corpse'.

Lie down on a firm surface, legs slightly apart, arms at your sides with the hands well away from the sides, palms turned upwards. Take a comfortable, leisurely breath, in and out, counting each out. Hold it until you feel the need to breathe in again. Unless you are exceptionally tense, it's difficult to go through ten of these cycles without losing count or even dozing off. But that, of course, is the object of the exercise.

To check your relaxation, if 'the corpse' doesn't work, tense and relax each of your muscles in turn, starting with the feet and working slowly and steadily upwards to the neck. Apart from its relaxing effect, this procedure is an interesting anatomical demonstration. The longer you can spend in the subsequent pose of total relaxation, the better: but

How to Relax

Yoga and the closely related Transcendental Meditation are both excellent relaxers: 'the corpse' (p.160) is especially effective, but hardly practicable at all times and places. The following routine, based on work at the Harvard Thorndike Memorial Library, is simple, effective and useful in the office, the plane, or anywhere else where you can or have to sit down.

1   After having a good stretch, sit quietly in a comfortable position, eyes closed.
2   Concentrate your *inner* attention on a fixed image or point: try the point between and above your eyebrows.
3   Deeply relax your muscles one by one, starting from the feet and working up the legs to the abdomen, chest, shoulders, neck and face; let the jaw muscles hang loose.
4   Concentrate on the breath passing deeply, easily and naturally through the nose, silently repeating the word 'one' (or any other neutral syllable, or a *mantra* if you've got one) every time you breathe out.
5   Adopt a passive attitude and allow yourself to relax easily and without effort. When distracting thoughts occur, refocus your attention on your breathing and the repetition of your neutral word.
6   If music helps, which is very likely, have it playing softly in the background. You can also try suggesting to yourself an increase in heaviness and warmth in your arms, hands and feet, possibly by using fantasy images of warm climates.
7   Continue for ten to twenty minutes; if you fall asleep, or drop into a doze, it doesn't matter. You're still relaxing.

The regular, rhythmic breathing is an essential part of the process. But there is also a yoga breathing technique which, while generally beneficial to the breathing apparatus, also has remarkable and mysterious relaxing properties:

1   Place the forefinger on the point between the eyebrows, thumb on one nostril, middle finger on the other.
2   Closing the left nostril, breathe in slowly and deeply through the right.
3   Closing the right nostril, breathe out slowly through the left.
4   Keeping right nostril closed, breathe in through the left.
5   Closing the left nostril, breathe out through the right.

Before a speech or some other taxing session, find a quiet place for this exercise. The relaxation will be immediate. Yogis use the following count for breathing: *in* to a count of three, *hold* for two, *out* to a count of six. But use whatever count suits you best as many times as you like.

you can manage very nicely without the corpse. You will find a ten-to-twenty minute relaxation course on page 161.

Those who are especially talented at relaxation experience a transformation of consciousness which is akin to a mystical adventure. Waves of beautiful colour pass across the closed eyes. The body seems to be floating in this brightly coloured space. The dreamer is awake yet not awake: in full control, yet outside normal consciousness. It's not at all surprising, in these circumstances, that the mystical value of the experience has come to be stressed far above the level of do-it-yourself mental therapy. To the true follower of yoga, the disciplines are the path to spiritual richness and development, the key to liberating the spirit from the prison of the body. True or false, the more ardently the faith is embraced, the more mental benefit yoga and its related enlightenment therapies will bring.

Only, remember the golden rule of self-development: moderation in all things. If you take the pursuit of any subordinate activity – whether it's physical fitness, karate, gambling or yoga – to the point where it ceases to be subordinate, but may even be dominant, you are changing the nature of your life priorities. There's the celebrated case of a great performer whose mysterious and terrible decline in technical prowess has coincided with an increasing dedication to the pursuit of Hatha Yoga. Perhaps it is just a coincidence; but perhaps it isn't.

Try reading any book on Hatha Yoga and you will find, as Arthur Koestler reports in *The Lotus and the Robot,* that much of it is horrible rubbish and, what's worse, completely incomprehensible. (So, incidentally, is much of that other mystical work, the *I Ch ing.*) Now, it remains true that, if the magic works, it doesn't matter whether it's nonsense (or whether I think it's nonsense) or not. The more proficient you are at yoga exercises, the greater the benefit you will obtain – and like many seemingly primitive and unscientific Asian practices (such as acupuncture), they do work (for yoga limbering up, see pages 163 and 164).

Yogis also lay great stress on breathing. The basic exercise involves breathing in through one nostril, out through the other, and then reversing the process. For some reason, this simple trick is deeply relaxing and is another anti-stress device. If you are feeling anxious or jumpy, a few minutes of breathing in this style should help to ease the tension. It's one way of employing the idle minutes which, we suggested earlier, a busy executive should build into his working day. And the yoga routines are incomparably good for limbering up the body, never mind what they do for the soul.

Drink and Cigarettes: Yes and NO

These natural methods of relaxation can be practised at odd

Limbering Up

The Surya Namaskar is the best limbering-up and spinal exercise known to man — as it should be, being several centuries old. Its translation is 'salute to the sun'; it is traditionally practised at dawn. Three Namaskars are excellent preparation for any exercise, or as stretching and spine-bending routines in themselves. Seven to twelve are the most non-Yogis should attempt.

	Movement	*Breathing*
1	Stand straight with feet together and palms together touching chest. Push feet downwards while stretching neck upwards.	—
2	Raise arms and bend backwards from waist.	In, deeply
3	Bend forwards from the hips. Keeping legs as straight as possible, place the hands on the ground by the sides of the feet at shoulder width, with face as close to the legs as possible.	Out, slowly
4	Stretch right leg back to full extent, leaving left shin vertical and keeping head back. Right foot on toes.	In
5	Place left foot beside right foot. Keep body in a straight line supported by toes and hands, looking up at horizon.	Hold
6	Lower body and rest toes, knees, chest, palms and forehead on the ground, keeping the stomach and pelvis off the ground.	Hold
7	Relax flat on the ground.	Out
8	Raise head and upper part of the trunk by extending your arms. Look up at the ceiling.	In
9	With feet flat on the ground, form an inverted V shape with the buttocks uppermost and the head between the arms, looking at the toes.	Hold
10	Bring the right foot forward leaving the left foot back — the mirror image of position four.	Hold
11	Bring the left leg up, place the feet together between the hands, straighten the legs and bring the face as close as possible to the legs. This is the same as position three.	Out
12	Bring your arms up and stretch them back, bending from the waist (the same as position two).	In
13	Straighten up, bringing the arms over the head and placing the palms together, touching the chest. This is the same as position one, and begins the next cycle.	

Five More Exercises

Five other useful, specific yoga-based exercises are for:
Neck and shoulders Sit crossed leg, lower head onto chest. Roll head to left, backwards, round to right. Raise head and look to right, then let head drop onto chest. Repeat in opposite direction. Perform whole routine twice.
Arms Stand with feet apart. Place fists together, thumbs underneath, elbows at shoulder height. Extend arms straight in front. Repeat six times.
Back Lie down, raise knees, feet flat on ground, arch back, then lower gently, one vertebra at a time.
Legs Lie down, legs extended. Raise both legs together until you are 'standing' on your shoulders, hands supporting the small of the back. Hold for count of five.
Ankles and calves. Sit with legs extended. Support left leg just off ground with hands under thigh. Rotate each foot through as large a circle as possible, 10 times in each direction. Repeat with right leg.

Three T'ai Chi Exercises

Always perform these movements slowly – as slowly as you can – and smoothly, with complete relaxation and easy breathing. Each movement starts from:
The neutral position: stand with your feet slightly apart, arms by your sides. Breathe out.
 1 Half clench your fists, with the backs of your hands facing the front, keeping the minimum tension. Breathing in, raise the hands almost to shoulder level, holding briefly before returning to the neutral position, while breathing out.
 2 Breathe in, raising the arms to the right while lifting the left leg, with knee bent, in front of you. When your arms reach shoulder level, kick gently forward, breathing in. Breathe out as the arms and legs go back to the neutral position. Repeat to left with the right leg.
 3 Breathe out and stretch out the left arm, bending the left knee and moving the right foot back along the ground, bringing the right arm up towards the left. Breathe in while bringing the left arm back towards the chest, simultaneously moving the left foot back alongside the right (which bears the body's weight during the movement) into the neutral position. Repeat with the left foot going back first.
There are 108 T'ai Chi exercises (or forms) in all. These examples will demonstrate the benefits of smooth and slow rhythmic movements (see *T'ai Chi: The Supreme Ultimate Exercise for Health, Sport and Self-defence* by Cheng Man-Ch'ng and Robert Smith, published by Tuttle, Tokyo, 1967).

Strains and Pains

If, despite the above, a muscle starts to hurt, the proper treatment, more often than not, is to continue to exercise it as much as the discomfort will allow. General relaxation will help to relax the stricken part: but immobility may well slow down rather than accelerate recovery.

Breathing Properly

It's also important to breathe **properly –** intercostal, diaphragmatic breathing, it's called. Here is how to establish it.

Method One

Lie on the floor and relax. Check that each part of the body, particularly the arms, shoulders and back, is not tense. Place one hand on the stomach, just below the end of the breast bone, and one hand on the lower ribs. Breathe in deeply and gently. During this in-going breath the ribs will rise outwards and upwards, followed by the stomach rising. Do this very **slowly.** Breathe out, and the stomach will descend followed by the ribs. Do this ten times slowly, feeling a definite separation between the movement of the stomach and the ribs. At first they may appear to work together, but with patience and concentration the separate movements can be developed.

It is important to remain calm and relaxed during this exercise. The exercise may be developed by gently sounding an OO sound as the air is expelled from the diaphragm and an AH sound when the ribs take over.

Method Two

Standing up, breathe in and raise the arms outwards and upwards until they are stretched above the head. The movement of the arms will assist the movement of the ribs and help to sustain them in a raised position during the second part of the exercise. While the arms are raised pant in and out three times. The stomach will move in and out. The arms should then be lowered slowly as further breath is exhaled.

The exercise may be extended by slowing the inspiration and expiration of the breath while the arms are raised.

These exercises are taken from *Clear Speech* by Malcolm Morrison, published by Pitman, 1977.

moments: not only at the desk, but waiting at the traffic lights, walking along (breathe in for three paces, out for four, hold for four), in airplane seats, and so on. If they keep your stress under control, there's another benefit: you won't be a customer for drugs. This isn't to insist that the ideal is to be a non-smoking teetotaller, since alcohol and nicotine are by far the most widely used (or widely supposed) antidotes to stress. But there would be a strong objection to cigarettes even if they didn't have the inconvenience of killing their addicts. They don't happen to suppress stress. In fact, by stimulating the action of adrenalin, they increase stress symptoms. In contrast, alcohol, provided it isn't consumed in addictive quantities, is remarkably effective and exacts a very small price in return for its benefits.

Most drinkers, however, even those who consider themselves moderate, wouldn't derive much benefit from what the doctors consider a moderate amount of booze. Modern research appears to confirm the old-established Anstie's Law. This limits the drinker to half a bottle of wine a day – which I would consider akin to total abstinence. It helps to follow rules: no drinks before noon, or until the sun is over the yard-arm (whenever that is – let's say six): no booze kept in the office or consumed while working. The idea is to drink only enough to help you relax and enjoy whatever you are doing – if you drink enough to get drunk, that's by definition too much. No longer are you drinking as an aid to living and as part of the joy of life – you're drinking for its own sake. That way disaster lies just as surely as it does for the two-pack-per-day smoker. Addiction or cancer are not acceptable alternatives to stress.

But the real drug problem is not these old faithfuls. The extent of addiction to alcohol can be checked (after which, so can the addiction itself, if necessary) by giving up liquor for a few days. If no withdrawal symptoms or insatiable thirst develop, then the situation is probably under control. The more difficult drugs, however, are those which have no sinister reputation and are not associated with any vice, social or otherwise – the hypnotic and tranquillizing medicines.

These have none of the psychic satisfaction of a glass of gin. But they are unquestionably powerful, in ways that their users, and even the doctors who prescribe them, don't understand. The power is less over the conditions for which the pills are taken than over the body. That is, it is characteristic for patients taking these drugs because they are depressed or unhappy to remain depressed and unhappy. Their mild doses of tranquillizers may tide them over from crisis to crisis. But the visible and invisible signs of severe stress and strain remain.

The power resides in the largely mysterious impact of these drugs on the central nervous system – the core of the super-computer. For instance, an overdose of Stelazine will produce in a healthy patient the symptoms of the appalling condition known as Parkinson's Disease. The fact that these pills look so innocuous and don't give the patient the kind of kick gained from Benzedrine or L.S.D. doesn't mean that they are harmless. Moreover, their use as a crutch removes the necessity for the over-stressed victim to lean on himself – to find either the cause or the cure of his overstrain, or both.

Any of the self-disciplines mentioned so far can help powerfully. Basically, this is because they all involve activity, and more activity (provided that it isn't more of the activity that has done the damage) is an excellent antidote: indeed, one study of neurotic patients found that they did at least as well on jogging as they did on tranquillizers. Even trivial activity can displace stress. Fiddling with the worry-beads beloved in the Balkans is remarkably soothing. Tidying the desk has the same effect. The principle is always the same – to calm the over-excited computer, either by putting it through simple routines which divert its attention, or by simply switching it off, as in meditation, or sleep (when it sorts itself out by dreaming), or by a rhythmic activity – music, or running, or controlled breathing.

The Insomniac's Charter

The therapeutic power of rhythm has been known for a long time. As usual, an unconsciously perceived truth has been embedded in folklore – in this case, the counting of sheep to assist in falling asleep. The metronomic effect of the counting itself, the rise and fall of the imagined sheep, perfectly illustrate the technique. Try lying comfortably in bed (say in the corpse posture), breathing in and out to a count of one, two; then holding the breath for a count of four. It should very rapidly lead to a partial or total escape from consciousness. Equally, it's difficult to stay awake with eyes closed while concentrating on breathing and counting each breath up to 100. You are highly unlikely to get more than halfway.

Veteran insomniacs will sneer at these and any other devices (hot drink before retiring, sleep masks, walks at bedtime, Aerobic conditioning, etc.) These will cure the normal sleeper who has an occasional or episodic difficulty. But your habitual insomniac is made of sterner stuff, and only sterner measures will suffice. Of these, the most effective is probably to accept the situation. Worrying about lack of sleep is as dangerous for the performance as worrying about sexual potency. In both cases, the cure is far more easily effected by ceasing to worry. You'll get an erection or orgasm again; and you'll get a good night's sleep. In the meantime, if their absence is causing no harm, why worry?

Where sex is concerned, other people are usually involved – and that may be the problem. But sleep is different; so long as you are functioning well in the day, with no signs of lassitude or nervous tension, you are by definition getting all the sleep you require. In fact, the architect Buckminster Fuller proved in a notable experiment that a subject can be trained to do with less sleep. He reduced his requirements to four hours a night. This would represent a 25 per cent increase in usable time for the normal sleeper – equivalent to an extra seventeen years on the three-score and ten. It would be silly to argue from the Bucky Fuller case – he is an exceptional man in many ways. But it's probably true that the super-computer will exert its best efforts to obtain as much sleep (and as much dream-filled sleep) as it requires.

If at all possible, then, sleep when you feel sleepy. If that is at some time and place other than between the sheets at night, so be it. Cat-nappers, as already noted, tend to believe that their brief afternoon sleeps have as much value as much longer night-time spells – and this could well be true. If the super-computer is short of dream-time, it will pack as much dreaming into the nap as it can. At night, unless the sleeper is catching up on a sleep debt (when dreaming is furiously intense), the super-computer can take its time, and long stretches of the night will pass without any mental activity other than the sluggish tide of beta rhythms.

If you can't get to sleep, or wake during the night and can't return to sleep, you have three alternatives.

(1) Use any of the above recommendations, or any patent methods of your own.

(2) Failing the above, or if they fail, take a pill.

(3) Get up, or switch on the light, and do something – if that something is sex (which, of course, could come under the first heading, too), it may facilitate the return to torpor.

The only alternative which needs elaboration is the pill. The newer hypnotics are preferable to the barbiturates, since the latter are both more dangerous and addictive. But the danger of psychological addiction exists with all sleeping pills. The victim begins to believe that he cannot sleep without a fix. Since belief is actuality in these matters, there he is – well and truly fixed: forced to go on indefinitely ingesting drugs which act directly and powerfully on the central nervous system, probably suffering some hangover effect every morning of his life.

Even some extraordinarily powerful minds have become hooked in this way. As noted earlier, Churchill couldn't sleep without barbiturates. Given that he also consumed vast quantities of alcohol, it's not surprising that the magnificent mind caved in so many years before the no less magnificent physique. The correct principle is to use the pills only when you can't sleep (not in case you can't); and to accept one or two sleepless or partially sleepless nights, if need be, to avoid developing a psychological dependence. The aim of developing mental and physical powers, after all, is to depend as deeply and widely as you can on those powers. Taking drugs does nothing for the self-control – and may do something harmful for the body and brain.

The most basic form of self-control, perhaps because it is so simple, is the hardest to apply. It cropped up in the consideration of business decisions. Just as it makes no sense to spend any time on a decision you don't have to take, or agonizing over a decision when you plainly have no alternatives, so it's foolish to worry over something that isn't going to happen for a long while, or may even not happen at all. The hedonistic philosophy of living for the moment has never been respectable, but in the control of stress, at least, it is eminently sound. If you have a serious professional or domestic problem, and the sun is setting over the oak tree in your garden, while the wine in your glass is a perfectly balanced Wehlener Sonnenuhr 1971, is the sunset less wonderful or the wine less delicious on account of your troubles?

Only if you let them be, is the answer. If the worried man concentrates instead on these supreme pleasures, or any other activity of the moment, the pressures of anxiety will be reduced at once. Moreover, many anxieties are of the unanswerable variety. To worry about losing your job (an anxiety to which even highly successful men are prone) is pointless, unless there's some course of practical action which will reduce the risk. Since you will then (of course) be concentrating on that action, it, and not the anxiety, will come to the forefront of the mind.

This could be called positive displacement: most techniques of stress control rely on displacement, on substituting some other action for the cause of the stress. But chewing gum, or rolling worry-beads, or even meditating are essentially negative. Of themselves, they accomplish nothing. Listening to music, another great relaxant, is positive, in the sense that it enlarges the mind. Massage improves the muscle tone; a sauna deep-cleans the skin, and the extreme dry heat, though it probably does nothing else for the system, certainly relaxes the muscles, while the associated rest eases the mind. But these are all beyond the real scope of self-management, since they require equipment and the aid of other people.

Sex Without Tears

Sex too can bring enormous relaxation and enjoyment. But since an overwhelming proportion of the problems that break up marriages and bring people to the psychiatrist's couch are sexual, it's clear that sex is capable of producing more strain and stress than it eases: for instance, over the vexed question of performance. Sexual powers, like any others involving the muscles and the mind, can be developed. The more intercourse a man has, the more his ability to make love is enhanced – and the process certainly works in reverse.

But Superman doesn't have to be a sex super-star. A male hasn't failed the manhood test because he can't come three times in an hour, or even a day for that matter. For neither man nor woman is it in any sense a failure not to have an orgasm. The most noted lover of post-war Europe, Aly Khan, was said to keep three gorgeous women enormously satisfied on three separate floors of a Paris hotel. His secret, allegedly, was that he had superb control over his orgasm, which he saved up until his day's round was complete. This control is a technique which, if it helps, can be quite easily mastered.

So long as your sex-life, whatever it is, satisfies you and your partner, if any, you are 'good' at sex. If it doesn't satisfy you, and the problem rests with you rather than your partner, it can quite possibly be cured. Horrendous problems like frigidity or inability to get or maintain an erection may be bread-and-butter jobs for a competent psychiatrist. Anyway, you don't actually have to have an erection to have sex, do you?

So, even in this most dangerous and stress-strewn minefield of human life, nothing is fixed, anything can be modified for the better. Stress is an inevitable accompaniment of striving, loving, succeeding, competing, working – all the virtuous activities. The trouble is that, without meaning to, the stressed person develops stressful habits – like eating too fast or sitting badly. The antidote is again to become increasingly conscious of the self and deliberately to correct the identified faults.

When you can, try moving with deliberate slowness – like 'a man walking through water', in the marvellous Chinese phrase. If you gobble or gulp, place the knife and fork on the table between each mouthful, put down the glass (as far away as you can) between each sip. Every such manoeuvre establishes command and control over the self. A dangerous condition of stress exists when the emotions and the hormones have control over you. This battle for power between the self as aggressor and as defender will last a lifetime. Perpetual victory for control will make that lifetime more worth living.

14. In Sickness and in Health

JUST as most men and women hanker after life everlasting, so do many seek eternal health (which comes to much the same thing, if you think about it). Vegetarians, yoga cultists, sunflower oil addicts, joggers, meditators – all tend to imagine that whatever pursuit turns them on will also keep up their physical vitality, if not for ever, at least well into what is generally known as old age. All of them, too, can find living or dead examples of amazingly . vital specimens of longevity who followed the cult in question. There are even Indians who believe in yogis whose diet consists entirely of water. None of these case histories proves anything about the cults in general; although they are very informative about the metabolism of the particular human being concerned.

The truth – not sad, but unavoidable – is that you can follow every precept in this book, or in any manual of self-improvement, or the teachings of every guru in India or the United States: but you may still be laid low by accident or disease, infectious or otherwise. Moreover, the greater success you and your organism have in surviving the years, the nearer you draw to the invariably fatal disease of old age. The super-computer and the super-machine end their amazing performances in a competition to see which one will wear out first, to establish whether mind and brain will fail in a reasonably fit and active body, or whether the computer will be left stranded on top of a body that will no longer obey instructions – because it cannot.

The sane objective is therefore not to avoid growing old, which is impossible, but to stay as fit as possible as long as possible. But fitness and health are not precise terms: not even as precise as death, over which there is now much medical controversy. If health is defined negatively, as the absence of any incapacitating pain or physical distress, that still leaves undefined the positive ability to do those things that you want to do, or might reasonably be expected to do: like walk a mile without collapsing from exhaustion. And are you healthy if you carry within

171

your body the incipient, as yet undetected worm of some unpleasant decay?

Such questions worry some people all of the time, others part of the time and a lucky few not at all. Those few are fortunate because they need no reassurance and can hope to be spared the physical ailments of the mind. While reassurance can easily be provided for the moderate or mild hypochondriac – for instance, in the shape of a complete physical check-up – the comforting dose must eventually wear off. Some loss of confidence, some anxiety about what might have happened since (or gone undetected during) the last check-up, will probably follow even if the patient has complete faith in such screening. The faith, in any case, may be misplaced: while this form of preventive medicine does catch a number of illnesses or conditions at an early stage, there's no evidence that the health of those examined, or their longevity, are much enhanced by the examination itself.

Preventive Behaviour – Not Medicine

If it throws up a high level of cholesterol and a low level of cardio-vascular fitness, and the patient is persuaded to change his or her life-style accordingly, then some benefit, even some marked benefit, may follow. But it's not the check-up, it's the change in life-style that is preventing deterioration – and even that is not certain. On average, the statement is true, though you may possibly be the fat fat-eater who drinks too much and takes no exercise, but who (probably thanks to good luck and marvellous heredity) confounds every rule. No man is an average. On the other hand, it seldom pays to buck the odds. If your mind needs the spur of an adverse medical report to stimulate it into more effective management of your material being, the medical examiners have undoubtedly earned their high fees.

All the same, the mind, not the medico, is the true key to the improvement. What applies to preventive medicine (a science which is still in its very early stages, since the genesis of much disease, not only cancer, is still so imperfectly understood) applies as strongly to medical treatment. In the Western world, the majority of patients seen by doctors in general practice have nothing wrong with them physically. They do have symptoms or complaints; but these are creations of the mind. Even in the case of some serious diseases, the causes are psychosomatic: the patient has literally 'made himself ill' – once again, an old phrase enshrines great truth.

Some clever idiots have argued from this truth that *all* illness is psychosomatic. The chapter on thinking should have helped to expose this nonsense. First, it is tautologous: since the possibility of an illness not caused psychosomatically is excluded by definition, no proof or disproof is possible. Second, even if it is true, so what? The fact that a sailor, in your daft view, has contracted psychosomatic scurvy is no reason for not topping him up, and that right swiftly, with Vitamin C. In other words, even if all disease were precipitated by the mind, it doesn't follow that the mind can cure its own material manifestations. It is true that a patient who wants to get better has more chance than one who doesn't; but that fact doesn't do away with the need for skilled professional treatment.

Whatever the origin, the symptoms are unpleasant – and remember that it's the symptoms that the patient wants to have relieved. Nobody would bother about an illness that had no symptoms: probably, they wouldn't even know it existed. There's an old gibe about doctors (and politicians, etc.) who treat the symptom and not the disease. This is a dreadful failing if the underlying disease will continue to run its devastating course, giving rise to still more and possibly worse symptoms. But in many circumstances treating the symptoms is perfectly sound practice. Skin complaints are frequently psychosomatic in origin, yet they can be more easily and effectively remedied by chemical treatment than by a course of psychoanalysis or by the practice of Hatha Yoga.

In any case, drawing a distinction between the doctor of the body and the healer of the mind is unsound. The great physicians have always known that they operate on both the machine and the computer. The placebo was an invention of doctors, not psychologists, and the harmless medicine has done much good down the ages in suppressing psychosomatic symptoms by the same route along which they arrived. In contrast, the powerful drugs have themselves created a whole new range of illnesses. They are in many cases poisonous; or they introduce alien substances into the body; or they disturb the normal bodily functions and balances; or by over-use they can create a new army of invading super-organisms.

This is the genuine doctor's dilemma of modern times. Advances in the chemistry of medicine mean that surgical procedures and drug therapies which would have been impossible before the Second World War are now commonplace. The trouble from the patient's point of view (and no other viewpoint counts, except in the case of communicable disease) is that much of the surgery and chemotherapy is unnecessary. Both trivial procedures like the removal of tonsils and major surgery like the excision of ovaries are performed far too often in cases where they are not needed at all. Antibiotics are administered as casually as cough medicine used to be, old people whose real trouble is lack of exercise have their systems undermined by inappropriate diuretics, and so on.

The typical patient, trained to regard his doctor with reverence, as some kind of high priest operating a confessional of the body rather than the soul, doesn't recognize that the doctor's dilemma is also the patient's. You can always refuse a treatment or discard a doctor and his advice. Only, most of us have too much awe and too much awareness of our own medical ignorance to do any such thing. Like putting all your trust in an investment adviser, because he knows about such matters and you don't, it's an abdication: wise if you are lucky, fatally foolish if you're not.

Doctors make mistakes, in which respect they are no different from the rest of us. The difference is that the doctor is expected to be nearly always right, partly because he is erroneously supposed to be the practitioner of a precise science. Not only does medical opinion turn round 180 degrees in a few years on vitally important matters (like the treatment of coronary victims by rest as opposed to exercise), but it can often swing right back again. Vast areas of uncertainty exist, and doctors vary greatly in their skill and their knowledge. In many cases, too, benign neglect is the best treatment available, but it isn't popular with the profession.

The Three Medical Possibilities

It isn't just that neglect earns no fees, or even that disuse (metaphorically) rusts the scalpel – though, if you are the world's swiftest hand at hysterectomies, you have a real need for wombs to remove. No: the problem can best be understood by the true story of a chief physician at one of London's great teaching hospitals. He advised a friend never to pass through its portals. As the physician pointed out, there are only three possibilities. Either the patient will get better; or he won't get better, but will survive; or he won't survive. In the third case, medical help is merely palliative. In the first case, it can only accelerate the process of natural cure; but in that case, and in the second, the hospital, with the best of intentions, can very easily make the patient worse – even unto the third and fatal condition.

Of course, the gloomy fellow exaggerated. Severe fractures won't get better unaided: the victim will survive, but will be a cripple for life, and there are plenty of other instances where skilled care can tip the balance between excellent recovery and a disaster. The point, however, is that the head physician in question wouldn't dream of applying his own prescription by turning away or refusing to treat a patient. Apart from the serious danger of a malpractice charge, there's the fact that all doctors are taught to recognize conditions and to treat them – taught, what's more, over an exceptionally long time and with greater than usual academic rigour.

So it goes against both the grain and the indoctrination to do nothing. If you go to a doctor, you are asking for treatment and will probably get it. So *you* must decide in the first instance whether you really need attention, and in the second whether, having received it, *you* really think it's good enough. Medical horror stories abound in every country. Within a month of writing these words, I heard of two such tales, one potentially fatal, one milder but equally illustrative. The first, from America, was of a woman whose dear and beloved physician, convinced that his patient was hysterical, resisted her admission to hospital until her undiagnosed infected gall bladder was three times its normal size. The other, from England, was of a man whose specialist correctly diagnosed a distressing nasal affliction, and proposed various unpleasant procedures for its treatment.

The American woman made the nearly fatal mistake of trusting her physician, even though she felt dreadful and was getting steadily worse. The Englishman, a tough-minded self-manager, couldn't understand why, after decades free of nasal problems of any kind, his condition had suddenly developed. The specialist wasn't much interested, but the self-manager persisted - and he found a possible answer. A year before, the family had bought a long-haired dog, which in winter formed the endearing habit of sitting by its master while he worked at his desk. In summer, when he worked outdoors, the condition disappeared. So the correct answer plainly had to do with either the dog or the outdoors - and no medical intervention was required.

The specialist in the case had used all his skill and learning, but he had not *thought* (which he hadn't been trained to do). The patient must think about his condition, even if he lacks the prime incentive of Americans, which is that any kind of medical treatment has now become so expensive. It's no wonder that some Americans are now carrying out routine medical procedures on themselves. Almost everybody has at some time or another used a clinical thermometer, though a surprising number of people are hazy about how to take their own pulses, or about what the results mean; but the idea of taking your own blood pressure or testing your own urine would have been unthinkable until quite recently. (For a simple self-guide to your risks of coronary heart disease, see page 176.)

It's a fact, however, that quite elementary procedures give the costly physicians running your check-up data through the computer a very large part of their essential information. The question of recovery rates was explored in Chapter 3. Take twenty minutes of strenuous exercise, like jogging or going briskly up and down stairs. Stop and rest; if your heart beat has fallen below 120 after five minutes and below 100 after ten minutes, there's a very strong presumption that your heart and lungs are in good working order. It may be that more elaborate procedures will discover some unsuspected disorder; but that isn't at all

Your Heart

The greatest health risk run by modern man is coronary heart disease (C.H.D.). You can estimate your own risk from this book on all but two counts – these two, which require medical examination, are:

1 raised blood pressure
2 serum cholesterol level
The others are:
3 obesity (see Chapter 4)
4 smoking
5 family history (see p. 183)
6 lack of exercise (see Chapter 3)
7 excessive stress (see Chapter 13)
8 predisposition in personality (below)

A guide to your exposure on 8 is your ambition rating on the test on p. 130, together with your fit with either the Type A or Type B personality (below).

Do you?. . .

1 feel a constant pressure to get things done?
2 often compete against the clock?
3 always hurry?
4 make decisions quickly?
5 get restless and impatient with being idle?
6 speak fast?
7 always arrive on time?
8 like to think about and do several things at the same time?
9 move, walk and eat rapidly?
10 often get impatient?
11 show the following physical characteristics in conversation?
    (1)   brisk and impatient body movements
    (2)   taut facial muscles
    (3)   fist-clenching
    (4)   explosive and hurried speech patterns
    (5)   lack of body relaxation
12 come out as ambitious in the test on p. 130?

The more of these questions you answer YES, the closer you are to the Type A pattern: the fewer, the closer to Type B, which has half the incidence of C.H.D. But Type A behaviour can be modified by deliberately adopting Type B norms – i.e., the opposite behaviour. (Meyer Friedman and Ray Rosenmann, *Type A Behaviour and Your Heart*) likely. And if you're that fit, you obviously don't need the spur to physical activity and sensible living that a medical check-up might otherwise provide.

Equally plainly, your own physical condition isn't an area where risks are permissible. When in doubt, seek advice. But try to follow the following simple rules:

1 Don't disdain the above simple indicators of good or bad condition, if you feel rotten. They will help to indicate whether there really is something wrong, or whether you are just feeling rotten – which does sometimes just happen.

2 If pain or other symptoms, in you or your loved ones, are especially uncomfortable or persistent, go to the doctor. Go even if you suspect that you are only being unduly anxious: anxiety is also a medical condition.

3 If anything significant or serious is diagnosed, find out as much as you can about the condition. Don't be fobbed off with technical language. Get it explained in words you can understand. You may not be a doctor, but it's still your body.

4 If you have the slightest reason for doubt or anxiety about diagnosis or treatment, after conducting your obligatory self-review of the situation, double-check with other professionals, whether that means medical family and friends or taking a second formal opinion. And *think* about what they say.

5 If things aren't going well, don't fall back on the argument that 'they know what they're doing.' Sometimes they don't. Again, seek information and apply thought and judgement.

6 If you have your own favourite remedies, and they seem to work, use them and don't be put off. This applies all the way from mustard baths for colds (although Russian research suggests contrarily that freezing the feet to minus 5 degrees Centigrade is far more effective) to such esoteric activities as acupuncture.

The Alternatives to Medicine

That raises a highly contentious subject: the use of what has been called 'fringe' or 'alternative' medicine, not to mention other fancier names. It's as well to be clear that none of these by-ways of medicine, some of them very ancient, is a cure-all. The late H.L. Mencken, in a devastating attack on chiropractic, observed that if somebody 'being ill

How Good is Your Back?

To test your spinal fitness, try the following six tests devised by Dr Hans Kraus and Dr Sonja Weber.

1   Lie flat on your back with your hands clasped behind your neck. Keeping your knees straight, raise your legs until your heels are 10 inches from the ground and hold for 10 seconds. This test shows the strength of your hip flexors.

2   Lie flat on the floor with your hands clasped behind your neck. Get someone to hold your ankles, then slowly roll up into the sitting position. This test shows the strength of your hip flexors and stomach muscles.

3   Lie flat on the floor with hands clasped behind the neck and knees bent. Again roll up into the sitting position while the ankles are held to the ground. This tests the strength of your abdominal muscles.

4   Lie face downwards, with a pillow under your stomach. With someone holding your pelvis and ankles, raise your trunk and hold for 10 seconds. This test demonstrates the strength of your upper back muscles.

5   Lie face downwards, with a pillow under your stomach. With a helper holding the small of your back, raise both legs and knees straight and hold for 10 seconds. This tests the strength of your lower muscles.

6   Stand with feet together and legs straight. Relax and slowly bend forward to touch the ground. If your finger tips fail to contact the ground with the knees straight it shows your back and hamstring muscles are too stiff.

How to Make Your Back Better

Failure to perform any of the Kraus-Weber tests 1-5 is a sign of muscle weakness. This can be corrected by repeating the test as an exercise. (To avoid the use of an assistant, the feet can be held steady by tucking them under a heavy piece of furniture.) Failure in test 6 is a sign of spinal stiffness. Back pain, though sometimes all but unendurable, doesn't have to be endured. The following under-five-minute routine will protect most backs against most troubles.

1   Sit on a chair with the feet apart; then bend down as far as you can between your knees. Breathe out as you go down; breathe in as you straighten up. Relax and repeat six times.

2   Kneel on the floor. Arch your back like a cat and let your head droop. Gradually reverse the position, raising your head and hollowing the back. Breathe out when your head drops, breathe in when the head is raised. Repeat six times.

3   Stand erect, legs straight and hands clasped behind your back. Slowly bend forward from the hips and apply the maximum possible stretch to your hamstring muscles. Breathe out as you flex forward, in as you straighten up. Repeat six times.

4   Stand erect and then gradually let the spine drop towards the floor. Do not apply force, but relax and let gravity do the work. Breathe out as you go down to touch the floor, breathe in as you straighten up. Repeat six times.

In addition to these exercises, it's advisable to observe sensible precautions in everyday life, such as:

1   If pushing a heavy load, use your back and **not** your arms to shove.

2   When lifting, keep the back straight. If you have to bend something, make it your legs.

3   Kneel, don't bend, to tasks below waist level.

4   Don't sit, especially for long periods, with crossed legs.

5   Get out of cars (and beds) by swivelling with legs together and placing both feet on the ground.

of a pus appendix submits willingly to a treatment involving balancing him on McBurney's spot and playing on his vertebrae as on a concertina', he (Mencken) for one was willing to believe that man was badly wanted in Heaven. The alternative therapists, like the orthodox ones, come in good, bad and middling varieties. But a good one will reveal his goodness, among other things, by refusing to treat conditions which are beyond his range.

That range is still enormous, especially for conditions, like backache, which often entirely defeat the resources of orthodox medicine. For decades medical professionals have resisted the enormous body of evidence which indicates that manipulation of the skeleton and muscles is highly effective in relieving conditions ranging from tension headaches to incapacitating pains in the lower back (which mankind has suffered from, usually under generic names like lumbago and rheumatism, since time immemorial). Many patients have been subjected to cruel and crippling surgery when manipulation would have healed them. Today quite a number of doctors have admitted osteopathy into the range of respectable treatments, yet many sufferers resolutely refuse to visit an osteopath as adamantly as they would decline the services of a faith-healer.

The only sense in their refusal is that such profound distrust will make them more difficult to treat. Thus the cycle turns again from the body to the mind. Osteopathy can achieve wonders of relief, and osteopathic advice can help greatly to avert the evil of back pain (see page 178). But the more you believe in a medical or quasi-medical practice the better, even if your belief is founded erroneously on anecdotes - on the cure of a terminal cancer patient by a course of acupuncture or the gift of sight to a blind man by the laying-on of hands. Miracles do happen, in orthodox medicine as in the unorthodox kind, without anybody knowing why. Bur miracles are by definition extremely rare; otherwise they would hardly be miraculous. The failures far outweigh the successes with the gravely sick. But if the talk of miracles strengthens somebody's faith in some far-out treatment of a minor condition, the mind is being reinforced in its fight against the failings of the body.

This basic truth must apply still more strongly to failings of the mind itself, usually before the onslaught of the autonomous emotional disturbances which range from neurosis to psychosis. Whatever therapy the neurotic patient chooses cannot succeed unless he believes in the therapy and the therapist. But this is a world of subjective convictions and non-existent data, where cures can take so long that it isn't clear whether the patient has been healed by the therapy or the mere passage of time, and where you don't have to be ill to be treated; after all, to call for help is to need it. When the call is answered, and the patient, say, spends expensive years in analysis, he isn't likely to emerge from the experience telling everybody that it was a waste of time and money.

To claim that an analysis was 'successful' is to state, no doubt proudly, that you are now a better and more integrated person, better able to cope with the strains and stresses of life. That may well be true, although such truths are difficult, if not impossible, to establish. But to feel better is to be better (we only know that people feel bad because they tell us, unless their physical symptoms are of the grossly obvious kind). So much the same lessons apply to the treatment of the super-computer. Far better, if you can, to avoid the need for treatment by preventive behaviour of the kinds described in this book. If the symptoms are highly specific, get the specific treatment at which mind-doctors are just as good as physicians. If in spite of everything your problems outrun your ability to cope, get help in which you can believe - and which you think works.

At least, you're unlikely to be killed by a psychiatrist. But panaceas, which are supposed to cure everything, can be the most dangerous treatment of all. The billionaire Howard Hughes undermined his health by crank eating habits; Christian Scientists have killed adored children by misplaced faith in the universal efficacy of prayer and Mother Nature. Pursue harmless health habits if you like. Dr Charles Glen King, a world authority on Vitamin C, links his habit of drinking tomato juice and eating oranges and lightly cooked broccoli sprinkled (the broccoli, not the oranges) with lemon juice and paprika with the fact that he hasn't had a cold for several years. He may be right, but it hardly matters if he's wrong – not so long as he likes broccoli. But there's no such thing as a 'health' food: only health eating, which requires a number of different foods, none of them with magical properties.

Health food addicts in the main do themselves no more harm than Dr King does with his broccoli and paprika. But basing your life to any extent on the pursuit of health for its own sake is somewhat pointless, like body-builders who develop muscles they will never conceivably need (except for winning male beauty contests). The super-computer and its attendant machine need good and careful maintenance, but only so that they can exploit their potential in other directions. Over the centuries, too, many thousands of people have contributed to an increasing body of knowledge which is slowly becoming more certain and which will help the Self to negotiate all manner of physical and mental crises. But the final answer, as always, must rest with the Self itself.

15.
As Old as you Feel

AS the previous chapter noted, the search for the key to long life is a general human preoccupation. It always has been, so that an English farmworker known as Thomas or Old Parr, who supposedly survived to 152, living in three centuries, is still commemorated on inn-signs 343 years after his death. Reports of Caucasians surviving well into their second centuries on diets consisting largely of yoghurt gain understandable credence. If the Caucasians can do it, why can't we? It's tough, in these circumstances, to be reminded that, although the average life expectancy of American men has risen from 63.6 years to 68.7 since 1945, and that of women from 68.7 to 76, the chances of reaching a very ripe old age have hardly improved at all.

The life expectancies at various ages are given in the table opposite. It contains actuarial facts about which you can do very little, save complain. But the objective shouldn't be to live longer (which isn't within mortal power to command); rather, it's to be fit for the duration, in every sense of fitness. That has been the whole intention of this book: its ideas lose none of their validity with advancing age, as various chapters have pointed out in many different contexts. Of course, you're going to get worse at some things, and not just at physical activities. For every DeWitt Wallace, who founded the *Reader's Digest* in 1922 and was still passing on major decisions in his eighties, there are many more veterans who are better out of the way - for everybody's sake.

That includes their own. In the first place, it's nonsense to refuse the opportunity, not of leisure, but of a different pattern of existence. In the second place, it's wrong and could be humiliating to hang on when powers have begun to fail and other, younger people are simply better at and more suitable for the job, whatever it is. This doesn't imply that the loss of powers is especially serious. People commonly exaggerate the extent of their inevitable decline. Dr Kenneth Cooper's age-corrected exercise charts show the precise degree of this deterioration in the most obvious instance of all, physical ability. Between the ages of 19 and 60-

Life Expectancy

YEAR BORN	MEN	WOMEN
1880-1900	35-40	37-42
1901-1910	48	51
1911-1920	$51\frac{1}{2}$	56
1921-1930	$58\frac{1}{2}$	62
1931-1940	$60\frac{1}{2}$	$66\frac{1}{2}$
1941-1950	65	$70\frac{1}{2}$
1951-1960	67	74
1961 onwards	$67\frac{1}{2}$	$74\frac{1}{2}$

This gives your basic life expectancy.

Present Age

1-4	1 yr	56-60	$6\frac{1}{2}$
5-20	2	61-65	8
21-25	$2\frac{1}{2}$	66-70	$9\frac{1}{2}$
26-35	3	71-75	$11\frac{1}{2}$
36-40	$3\frac{1}{2}$	76-80	12
41-45	4	81-85	$6\frac{1}{2}$
46-50	$4\frac{1}{2}$	86 plus	$4\frac{1}{2}$
51-55	$5\frac{1}{2}$		

Add this figure to basic life expectancy to get your present expectancy after also adding one year for each five-year period your father lived or has lived past 70. Do the same for your mother.

Marital status: If you are married, add five years. If over 25 and not married, deduct one year for each unmarried decade.
New Total..........years.
Where you live: If in a small town add four years. If in a city, subtract two years.
New Total..........years.
Economic status: If wealthy, or poor, *most* of your life, deduct three years.
New Total..........years.
Your shape: If you are over 40, deduct one year for every 5 lb (2.25 kg) you are overweight. For each inch (2.5cm) your girth measurement exceeds your chest measurement, deduct two years.
New Total..........years.
Exercise: Regular and moderate, add three years; regular and vigorous, add five years.
New Total..........years.
Disposition: Good-natured and placid, add one to five years; tense and nervous, subtract one to five years.
New Total..........years.
Alcohol: Heavy drinker, subtract five years; very heavy, subtract ten.
New Total..........years.
Smoking: 10-20 cigarettes per day, subtract three years; 20-30, subtract five years; more than 30, subtract ten years; pipe or cigar, subtract two years.
New Total..........years.
Family environment: Regular medical check-ups, regular dental care, add two years. Frequently ill, subtract two years.

Example: Year born (man) 1931	=	$60\frac{1}{2}$
age in 1978 is 47	=	$4\frac{1}{2}$
father and mother 75	=	2
other scores (net)	=	0
predicted age of expiry		67

FINAL TOTAL..........years.

plus, the standard of superior performance over a distance of 1.5 miles declines by 30.5 per cent. Between 30 and 60 the decline is 12.5 per cent. From the age of 40 (which for no very clear reason is often called 'the prime of life') the falling-off to 60-plus is only 7 per cent. But there is, of course, an overriding condition: that the man concerned exercises to maintain his fitness.

Practice Makes Performance

What rules for running governs other faculties as well. In 1977 the British competition to find the B.B.C.'s Mastermind was won by a retired ambassador in his sixties, who achieved the amazing feat of answering twenty hard general knowledge questions correctly in the space of two minutes. Bear in mind that each question has to be read out during that 120 seconds, and the remarkable performance of this sexuagenarian mind is clear. It's doubtful whether it could have been outdone by a brain of any age. The chapter on memory noted that failing powers owe more to disuse than to decrepitude. How far elder people do invariably suffer from great difficulty in recall, especially of immediate facts as opposed to past memories, is hard to establish. But aged academics have long been famous for their incredible memories for facts and faces - largely because they keep those memories in practice.

The absent-minded professor is literally that. He doesn't remember where he left his car, or his wife, because his mind has been concentrating on something else, such as the transcription of Assyrian epitaphs, and he hasn't actually noticed what he has been doing. Everybody is guilty of the same failing. In Chapter 14 you were advised, for the sake of your back, always to leave a car in two-legged style, not leading with one leg first. Try to adopt this habit, and see how many times in the first couple of weeks you find yourself outside the car with no certain recollection of how you emerged, or else balanced unstably on the one leading leg. Your mind was simply engaged elsewhere, an attribute which has nothing to do with age but much to do with the mechanics of the mind.

Not only phenomenal memories, but super-normal strength can last long after the three-score-and-ten mark. Very few octogenarians would be able to emulate Charles Atlas by tearing telephone directories in half, or to copy the great wrestler George Hackenschmidt by jumping fifty times over the back of a chair. But then, very few people of any age can perform either feat. The requirement is to maintain your performance as near as you can to whatever level is satisfactory. For Atlas and Hackenschmidt that happened to mean strong-man acts of quite awe-inspiring dimensions. But walking three miles in an hour at the age of 70 is not only more feasible but, if practised every day, will go a long way towards maintaining agility. In 1977, indeed, the Scottish runner, Duncan Maclean, covered 100 metres in 21 seconds at the age of 92.

Don't Accept Degeneration

While these known facts are especially striking in the context of great age, they become important much earlier in life. The mid-life change - which in my case partly prompted the writing of this book - is undeniably a widespread phenomenon. Dr Cooper has noted his surprise in finding that the majority of the participants in his Aerobics programmes were not the youngsters he had expected, but men and women over 40. These people had sensed the fact, or responded to the reminder, that without exercise their physical decline would accelerate after 40. But the Aerobics enthusiasts are in a minority, even in the United States, where exercise programmes and improved diet and health habits (like not smoking) are what have succeeded recently in producing a significant rise in male life expectancy. In all countries most people are content to accept not decline, but degeneration - that is, a faster than necessary falling away in their performance.

It may be that this degeneration is not recognized, or that the subject is content to accept his or her physical condition because the faculties which are being exercised (like professional skills) are in fine fettle. The choice is legitimate, although there's some analogy with the obese fellow who won't diet or exercise because there's apparently nothing wrong with him, he can work as hard as anybody, and he enjoys his food and drink. He is still almost certainly functioning below potential and without a doubt he is running unnecessary risks. Just so do chain-smokers defend their deadly habit by pointing out that you can be killed just as easily crossing a road: too true, but you still wouldn't run across a motorway in the rush hour without looking to left or right.

The Self has the divine right, within limitations, to choose what it wants itself to be. Managing yourself, or making maximum use of an effectively unlimited potential, is simply a way of making that choice more rewarding. Take the simple example of sex. Like Thurber's bear in the backroom with his booze, you can take it or leave it alone. Those people with vigorous and happy sex-lives have a pleasure anf an outlet which celibates and those in the various in-between categories are denied - or which they deny themselves. So long as the latter are happy, or at least don't care, it doesn't matter. But it is important when somebody who would actually prefer to have sex enjoys (or doesn't enjoy) a diminishing love-life because of advancing age.

The reason of age is simply spurious, and the jokes about old or even middle-aged men who can't do it any more are in truth terribly sad. All the evidence shows that in the overwhelming majority of cases, given the

185

will, regular activity and an acceptable partner, love-making, like vigorous walking, can and does last long past the seventy barrier. Old Thomas Parr was still at it in his hundreds. Genuine physical impotence appears to be extremely rare. If you lose interest, of course, your performance will fall away, at any age. But that loss of interest is a function of the mind, not the body, and it undeniably results in a loss of enjoyment as well.

So it's a harmful myth to think of men and women who enjoy sex, and plenty of it, in their later years as Superlovers; they have simply kept their sexual faculties intact by using them. Another myth, incidentally (also enshrined in a host of dirty stories), is that sexual activity is physically risky for the aged. In fact, cardiac patients are best advised to resume their sex-lives, if any, as soon as they can walk around a room - although presumably the more acrobatic variations wouldn't be suitable at this stage of the game.

It's all another example of the key to all super-performance. The general truth is that practice doesn't make perfect, because perfection, where it does exist, is usually a gift of the gods: for most people, in most of their activities, the perfect is always out of reach, no matter how much they improve. But life is practice, anyway, and the best practitioners are those who practise most – at all ages. The older you get, the more important it is to practise to maintain your prowess within the range of that mental or psychological age which governs your attitude to life. That's what is meant by another old saw, that you are as young as you feel. Physical age is an ineluctable, unmanageable fact; but the level of performance is something that can be managed.

Life is a long journey that takes a short time. For most of that passage, the super-computer and the super-machine serve their master, the Self, fantastically well, and serve it better if the Self chooses to demonstrate its mastery. The machine has to eat and drink, and it takes exercise of a sort in any event. It might as well take these activities seriously and do them efficiently. The computer, too, will never stop its routines. The faculties of absorbing and presenting information, of arranging and encoding material, of working through alternatives and examining possibilities, of digesting experience and making use of the results – these continue day in, day out. These routines, too, are performed better if they are carried out consciously.

The use of time, like the employment of language, is among those continuous routines: both are also among the most obvious examples of how the routines can be improved by taking thought. These are, however, the easy areas: the conscious ones, where deliberate thought can be directed towards chosen ends without much chance of outside or damaging interference. But the influence of other people and one's own unconscious self can never be excluded. Thus the more complex areas of

186

self-management, in which the desired results can never be guaranteed, are those where these two influences the external and the internal - often have the decisive voice.

But self-control can rule in relations with other people, individually or in the mass; ambition, personal and financial, can be brought under the regime of reason. You can learn to live with and adapt to stress and the troubles of the body, even the inevitability of ageing. None of these processes can be accomplished with the ease and finality of speeding up your reading. But advances can be made and small victories won: for instance, by making the cultivation of new and different activities a rule of life, you can make a virtue of the human vice of gushes of enthusiasm followed by the onset of boredom. This vice afflicts whole societies as well as individuals. In a nation the process of changing social tides produces regeneration. The same thing happens to the individual, who doesn't have to be young to develop a new passion for roses or horse-riding - or even both.

On reflection, the creator of Superman wasn't being fanciful nearly four decades ago when he made his creature faster than a speeding bullet, more powerful than a locomotive and able to leap tall buildings at a single bound. Through his technology, man has mastered all these abilities and many more, reinforcing with gadgets every one of his inborn faculties, even memory. The immediate playback of a goal or some other sporting incident is nothing but the provision of an artificial memory which is much more reliable than even a highly trained human brain. Yet the artificial memory is no less human for that: it is still a human creation. These and the other artefacts of the twentieth century have not robbed the individual of his dignity: they have given in-dividual man far greater scope than ever before to express and to manage the individual condition. By good fortune, the technological advance has been accompanied by considerable development in knowledge of the extraordinary combination of mental and physical powers which created the technology. Put the two together, and the result won't be Superman or Superior Man, but the best which any human being can hope to achieve Super-Self.

Select Bibliography

This is not a complete list of all the sources used in compiling this book, or of all the works which might broaden readers' understanding of the self-management techniques mentioned. They are the books which in one way or another I have found both useful and entertaining in my journey around the Self.

Body

DEVON, David: *Hands for Healing* (London 1966)
    The answer to those who think manipulation is quackery
ILLICH, Ivan: *Medical Nemesis* (London 1975)
    A highly cautionary tale about modern medicine
NORFOLK, Donald: *Habits of Health* (London 1977)
    Sound general advice on how to help the body stay healthy
SMITH, Anthony: *The Body* (Harmondsworth 1970)
    An exhaustive but far from exhausting guide to everything
WRIGHT, Beric, and BAILEY, Alan: *Executive Ease and Disease* (Glasgow 1976)
    A Longer Life (London 1977)
    Useful summaries on health and ill-health habits

Communication

GOWER, Sir Ernest: *Complete Plain Words* (Harmondsworth 1970)
    The classic on the subject, now as always
MORRIS, Desmond: *Manwatching* (London 1977)
    Glossy but amusing study of the non-verbal.
MORRISON, Malcolm: *Clear Speech* (London 1977)
    As brief and as lucid as a good speech itself should be
ORWELL, George: *Collected Essays* (London 1961)
    The writing is as good a piece of teaching as the lessons

Diet

AGER, Anne: *The New Carbohydrate Counter* (London 1974)
Indispensable for the low carbohydrate dieter
CAMERON, Robert: *The Drinking Man's Diet Cookbook* (London 1970)
Basically, Yudkin plus booze for those who want their drinks
STILLMAN, Dr Irwin, and BAKER, Samm Sinclair: *The Quick Weight-Loss Diet* (London 1970)
Contains all the diets you could possibly ask for
YUDKIN, Dr John: *This Nutrition Business* (London 1976)
Useful supplement to diet book for would-be home nutritionists
This Slimming Business (Harmondsworth 1970)
An excellent and brief guide to the low carbohydrate system

Emotion

BERNE, Eric: *Games People Play* (Harmondsworth 1970)
More stimulating than useful: the start of a major trend
HARRIS, Thomas: *I'm OK - You're OK* (London 1973)
All you want to know about the popular face of TA
JACOBSON, Edmund: *You Must Relax* (London 1977)
For non-mystics, an eminently sane and convincing guide
NORFOLK, Donald: *Executive Stress* (London 1977)
The best practical book written on the subject
BLOOMFIELD, Harold, *et al.*: *TM: Discovering Inner Energy and Overcoming Stress* (London 1976)
The most successful of the Asian quasi-mystical imports
SELYE, Hans: *Stress without Distress* (London 1975)
The classic work on a classic syndrome of modern man

Exercise

COOPER, Kenneth: *Aerobics* (London 1970)
The New Aerobics (London 1970)
The Aerobics Way (New York 1977)
These three books are the exercise gospels
KINGSLAND, Kevin and Venika: *Complete Hatha Yoga* (London 1976)
The full yoga works - but unusually clearly and well presented
MAN-CH'NG, Cheng, and SMITH, Robert: *T'ai Chi* (Tokyo 1967)
For those who want routines even less physically demanding than yoga
MARSHALL, Lyn: *Wake Up to Yoga* (London 1976)
The least pretentious and most useful of the yoga guides

Management

DRUCKER, Peter: *The Effective Executive* (London 1970)
   One of the master's most masterful and invaluable works
GELLERMAN, Saul: *Managers and Subordinates* (London 1976)
   Behavioural science brought down to earth
HELLER, Robert: *The Naked Manager* (London 1974)
   Modesty forbids: it's a debunking survey of the whole field
LAKEIN, Alan: *How to Get Control of Your Time and Your Life* (London 1974)
   Full of useful advice, though not great literature
McKINSEY, J: *Anthology: Arts of Top Management* (New York 1970)
   Important collection of essays covering the key subjects
TOWNSEND, Robert: *Up the Organization* (London 1971)
   Another debunking exercise, written from the inside
WOOD, E.: *Bigger Profits for the Smaller Firm* (London 1972)
   A careful guide to a subject very rarely touched upon in books

Mind

Mind

BERNE, Eric: *Transactional Analysis in Psychotherapy* (London 1975)
   Further reading for the T.A. interested
BUZAN, Tony: *Advanced Reading and Learning Manual* (Brighton 1977)
   Make the Most of Your Mind (London 1977)
   Speed Memory (London 1977)
   Speed Reading (London 1977)
   Use Your Head (New York 1977)
   All these books are excellent guides to mental management
CAMPBELL, Robert: *The Enigma of the Mind* (London 1977)
   Glossy, pop account of what's known to date
HUGHES, Patrick, and BRECHT, George: *Vicious Circles and Infinity* (London 1976)
   Brief but stimulating guide through the complexities of paradox
ROSE, Steven: *The Conscious Brain* (London 1973)
   Does for the mind what *The Body* does for the body
SMITH, Adam: *Powers of Mind* (London 1976)
   A funny but instructive romp through the mental therapies